Amma Ampong Agyeman-Prempeh is a certified bookworm. She shares her love for reading and writing on www.bookwormgh.com. She enjoys reading (auto)biographies – an opportunity to walk into another's shoes if even for a brief moment.

After completing Wesley Girls' High School in Cape Coast, Ghana she went on to study for a Bachelor's Degree in International Relations and French (with Honours) from Calvin College in Grand Rapids, Michigan, USA and a Master's Degree in International Relations from University of Warwick, UK. She lives in Accra, Ghana with her family.

DEDICATION

This book is dedicated to my son, Yaw Agyeman-Prempeh. Thanks for this incredible gift of motherhood.

• *KEEPING THE BALANCE SERIES* •

Motherhood 101

A memoir of my experience as a newlywed juggling pregnancy/motherhood, marriage, work and a social life

Amma Ampong Agyeman-Prempeh

DAkpabli

DAKPABLI & ASSOCIATES
ACCRA

MOTHERHOOD 101

ISBN: 978-9988-2-7618-8
ABAVANNA SERIES (AV6)

Edited by James Anquandah

Cover Design and Book Layout by
Nene Buer Boyetey
P O Box NM 78, Nima, Accra, Ghana
Email: nene@bigglesglobal.com
Tel: +233 302 333 502 | +233 244 634 204

Cover Illustration by Fleance Forkuo

Published by
DAkpabli & Associates
P O Box 7465, Accra North, Accra, Ghana
Email: info@dakpabli.com
Tel: +233 264 339 066 | +233 244 704 250 | +233 247 896 375

ACKNOWLEDGEMENTS

I am grateful to my husband, Yaw Sarpong Agyeman-Prempeh. Thanks for sharing the experience of parenting with me.

I thank my mother, Mrs Mary Aboagye, for encouraging me to write. Since high school, she has urged me to write a book about my experiences. Ma, thanks for your confidence in me, and for believing that I have a story worth sharing.

I am grateful to my father, Judge Kwaku Aboagye, for being a hands-on father and for giving me a remarkable childhood.

To my sister, Yaa Gyamera Aboagye, you are an amazing person! Thank you for being a mother to my son. He loves you just as much as you love him.

Thank you, Joshua Senavoe, for helping me put my very first draft together.

INTRODUCTION

This book, *Motherhood 101*, the first of its kind in Ghana and Africa, is a memoir of my experience as a first-time mother.

In this book, I bare it all – the Good, the Bad and the Ugly! Motherhood is undoubtedly an amazing experience, but it is also very challenging. There are moments of indescribable joy, and there are also times of heart-wrenching pain. For me, the most difficult aspect of motherhood is having to combine being a mother with my other equally important roles of being a wife, daughter, sister, friend, church member, career woman, entrepreneur, among others.

This book is not a rant. No! Far from that! I enjoy being a mother and I will not trade motherhood for anything in the world. I am blessed with a loving family that has been supportive throughout this journey. However, the story will not be complete if I do not share the frustrations and disappointments I have experienced as I struggle to keep the balance between motherhood and all my other roles.

I do not claim to be an expert. I am simply a mother telling her story. Learn from my experience. Laugh at my mistakes. Live through my stories. Motherhood is all about learning on the job.

Chapter One

MUMMY-IN-WAITING

For as long as I can remember, I have been intrigued by pregnancy and motherhood. As a child, I used to play in front of the mirror and pretend to be pregnant. I would roll up clothes into a ball and fasten it under my dress as my "bump". With the classic hand-on-waist pose, I would walk round the room acting like a pregnant lady. I couldn't wait to be pregnant!

As I grew older, I looked forward to motherhood with eager anticipation. I would be the pregnant fashionista with trendy clothes, whether at the office or out on a date. I would live a 'normal' life – working full-time, taking care of my home, and having fun with my husband. And after childbirth, I would strike the perfect balance to juggle roles as a wife, mother, and professional.

Sure, I knew that motherhood would be challenging, but I was optimistic that those challenges would be few and far between. I was positive that being a mother would bring me incredible joy and a sense of fulfilment.

My first experience with taking care of babies and toddlers was at the church crèche when I was 15 years old. Caring for children came naturally to me and I connected easily with these little ones. I would feed them, change their diapers and play with them. When my first niece, Jessie, was born in 2007, I was overjoyed! She was the first grandchild of my parents, and we were all excited. Three years later, my second niece, Marie, was born, and with two adorable little girls came double the excitement. I couldn't wait to give them a cousin to play with.

When I got married in October of 2011, I knew that I wanted to have children right away. However, it was not a do-or-die affair for me or us. I was aware that having a child so soon after getting married could also be overwhelming, so I was open to a few months' delay to help us adjust to married life. I didn't want my desire to have a child to consume me, so I tried to keep both points of view in mind.

I must admit, though, trying to keep this balance wasn't always easy. I wanted to have a baby as soon as possible. I didn't want to wait. With all the talk about fertility declining with age, I didn't want to take any chances. I wanted to start trying early so that even if it didn't happen immediately, I wouldn't end up losing too much time in the process.

So, barely a few weeks after our honeymoon, I was already dying to find out whether I was pregnant or not. My husband teased that he could sense I was already pregnant, but I laughed it off. I didn't want to get my hopes high so soon. One day, on my way home from work, I purchased a home pregnancy test kit to put an end to the suspense. Two red lines meant you were pregnant and if you weren't, a single red line appeared. As I waited anxiously for the lines to appear, I secretly hoped for the former but hedged my emotions. I didn't want to be disappointed. A few seconds went by and I mustered the courage to look. I opened one eye slowly, then the other. From the corners of both, I saw one line, and then two – two bold red lines! Yessss! I was pregnant!

I was overjoyed! God had answered my prayers. In fact, He had exceeded my expectations. I was simply elated. I could barely stop myself from posting a picture of the positive pregnancy test on my Facebook page, but I knew I had to tell my husband first. This was a dream come true. I was going to be a mummy. I was going to have my own child. My very own baby!

I couldn't wait for my husband to get home to share the good news. I was bursting with excitement. I wondered what his reaction would be. Everything had happened so fast and it would make perfect sense for him to be anxious, but I prayed that he would be just as happy as I was. Thankfully, he was! And we were both excited that we were going to be parents.

Chapter Two

ANTENATAL CLINIC I

Now that the pregnancy had been confirmed, I needed to see a doctor for a full check-up. My sister recommended her doctor, and off I went to the hospital all by myself. After a few questions, the doctor informed me that he would perform an ultrasound scan. But before he could go ahead with the scan, he advised me to drink a lot of water to the point where I felt I needed to pee. "Easy enough", I thought to myself. I went back to the reception and helped myself to several cups of water from the dispenser. After what felt like an hour, but was probably 15 minutes, I felt the urge to pee. But guess what? The doctor was attending to someone else! I couldn't believe it. My bladder was about to burst. I waited patiently till I finally had my turn. The doctor then escorted me to the ultrasound scan room.

It was surreal. First, the doctor applied some cold gel over my abdomen, then poked around my lower abdomen with a probe. After a few pokes, he pointed at what looked like a dot on the screen. That was the embryo. That was my baby. It was really true that I was going to have a baby. It was a very special moment for me.

During the ultrasound scan, the doctor took some measurements of the embryo on the screen and typed some comments. He informed me that I was six weeks pregnant. Six weeks pregnant? How was that possible? I had been married for barely three weeks, yet I was six weeks pregnant? How was I going to explain that to anyone? It was then that he told me that the 'age' of a pregnancy starts from the first day of the last menstrual period. That means that, by that measure, I was technically already three weeks pregnant on my wedding day, though I actually was not. Go figure!

I was very happy to hear that I was indeed pregnant and that the baby was well and located in the right place, too. On my way home that afternoon, I'm sure I was grinning ear to ear. I couldn't believe I was going to be a mother. Whenever I was caught in traffic, I would take another look at the print-out from the ultrasound scan. I was truly in a happy place .

Chapter Three

NOVEMBER 2011 - ROUGH START

I took it for granted that I would be able to continue with my normal activities throughout the pregnancy. I didn't want to slow down at work just because I was pregnant. No! Not me! I had heard it being said many times that, "pregnancy is not a disease", so I didn't want to be a slacker. Unfortunately, I learned the hard way that although pregnancy is not a disease, sometimes, pregnant women need to slow down and take it easy.

On 12th November 2011, when I was barely seven weeks pregnant, I was part of the organisers of a graduation ceremony for our students. The programme was extremely chaotic. The challenges seemed endless- graduands arriving late, gowns with no matching caps, insufficient seating (some graduands came along with bus-loads of people), a late MC, and a host of other challenges. At the end of the day, everything worked out well, but I was well and truly exhausted. A few days later, I started to feel some cramping in my lower abdomen. I ignored it initially as I assumed that was all part of pregnancy.

But when it persisted, I told my mother about it and she insisted that we go to the hospital to check it out.

At the hospital, the doctor performed another ultrasound scan and confirmed that the 'Baby' was fine. However, he was concerned that I was under too much stress from my job, and its accompanying three-hour daily commute. He recommended that I stay at home for the rest of the first trimester. Miscarriages were most likely to occur during that time, he explained, so he wanted me to be extra careful.

What? Stay at home for six weeks? I couldn't believe it! What would I do during that time? What about all the work I had to do at the office? How frustrating! There was so much more I wanted to do besides staying home. I had a husband to go on dates with, friends to hang out with, work to do at the office, church programmes to participate in, and social events to attend. Sleeping and lazing about on the couch were definitely not on my schedule.

I'm a workaholic so staying at home was going to be tough. But I had no other option. I needed to put my Baby first. So, I simply had to follow the doctor's order.

From the hospital, I went back to the office to pack my stuff. I didn't say anything to my colleagues about being put on partial bedrest. Indeed, I had not even told them yet that I was pregnant. So, I simply told them I was taking a few days off because I wasn't feeling well. That day, for the first time since I got married, someone else drove me home. That was the beginning of my 'solitary confinement'.

Fortunately, staying at home was not always as bad as I had imagined. Indeed, it was good to be able to relax and slow down for a few weeks. Work kept me so busy that I didn't have time to truly enjoy my home. I was always on the go - leaving home before 6:00 am to beat traffic and getting home after 5:00 pm. My partial bedrest gave me a chance to rest, read, and to experience what it was like to be at home during the daytime.

Being at home also gave me an opportunity to read my Bible and pray more. I prayed for my Baby. I prayed that he or she would stick around for the nine months. One of my favourite Bible verses was Numbers 6, verses 24-26: "The Lord bless you and KEEP you, the Lord make His face to shine on you and be gracious unto you. The Lord turn his face toward you and give you peace". This became my personal prayer for my Baby.

I researched the various names of God, put them together in one document, printed it out, and stuck it in my Bible. These names gave me great comfort. Knowing that God had been there for others in the past, assured me that He would also take care of me. He was my El Shaddai (The All-sufficient One); Jehovah Jireh (The Lord will Provide); Shalom (The Lord is Peace); Shammah (The Lord who is Present);

Jehovah Rapha (The Healer); and El Roi (The God who sees Me).

I also spent time on YouTube listening to inspirational gospel songs. I fell in love with the Soweto Gospel Choir from South Africa. My top two favourite songs from their collection were "Oh It Is Jesus" and "Khumbaya".

Oh It Is Jesus

Oh it is Jesus
Yes it is Jesus
It's Jesus in my soul
For I have touched the hem of His garment
And his blood made me whole

Khumbaya

Somebody's crying Lord, Khumbaya
Somebody's praying Lord, Khumbaya
Somebody's crying Lord, Khumbaya
Somebody's praying Lord, Khumbaya

O Lord hear my prayer, Khumbaya
As I lift my voice and say, Khumbaya
I need you Lord today, Khumbaya
I need you right away, Khumbaya

Somebody's crying Lord, Khumbaya
Somebody's praying Lord, Khumbaya

Somebody's in despair
Somebody feels like no one cares
I know you'll make a way
Yes, Lord you'll make a way

Oh Lord, Khumbaya
Oh Lord, Khumbaya
Oh Lord, Khumbaya

When I wasn't praying or singing, I spent time reading, watching TV, listening to the radio, and surfing the internet. Sometimes, I felt strong and would push myself to do some household chores. But the cramping would quickly remind me why I was on partial bed rest. How frustrating!

My favourite TV channel was the Food Network. Unsurprisingly, watching all those cooking shows often stirred up all sorts of cravings within me. Sadly, most of the foods I craved were not even readily available in Ghana. I craved Mexican food from Qdoba and crab rangoons from Golden 28, a Chinese restaurant in Grand Rapids, Michigan. And even though I couldn't always satisfy my cravings, I gave myself special treats without feeling guilty. After all, I was eating for two .

The hardest part about being put on bed rest was that I missed some significant family events. I missed my father's birthday. I missed my mother's birthday. And I also missed my niece, Marie's one-year birthday bash (You know those first birthdays are really for the grown-ups anyway). I felt left out. Life was going on fast all around while I was stuck at home.

Sometimes, I felt lonely being all by myself at home. My husband was combining a full-time job and a full-time Master's programme, so he was quite busy. Thankfully, my mother made my days of solitary confinement more bearable. She would leave the office to come and keep me company at home. And when she was too busy to visit, she would send someone else to bring treats – Papaye, fruits, you name it. She also brought us home-cooked meals so that I always had enough food at home. And to top it all off, she would do my grocery shopping for me every week. She made sure that I didn't have to lift a finger.

If I was trying to keep my pregnancy a secret, then staying at home was not helping at all. People began to question why I was at home and not at work. I felt like a slacker. I knew I didn't have to explain to everyone why I was at home. But for the few who knew about the pregnancy, I didn't want them to think I was lazing around at home just because I was pregnant. I wished they could understand the potential complications I could suffer if I didn't take it easy. I just prayed for the days to go by quickly so that I could graduate to the second trimester of pregnancy. I couldn't wait to have my life back again and to resume my normal schedule.

Chapter Four

DECEMBER 2011 – CHRISTMAS INDOORS

December is usually full of celebrations, and the December of 2011 was no exception. The month was ushered in with my husband's birthday on its first day. It was our first birthday celebration as a married couple, and I was determined to make it special. I defied my doctor's orders and worked my butt off to cook a special birthday meal. I wasn't going to let his birthday go without any celebration. The day after Yaw's birthday was a public holiday so a few of his friends came over and we continued the birthday celebration. I knew I was in trouble when during the late afternoon I began to feel some cramping in my lower abdomen, but as I didn't want to ruin the joyful moments, I kept it to myself and suffered in silence. It was frustrating. Had I become so frail that I couldn't even survive a few hours of cooking?

I missed my mother's birthday celebrations on 12th December. The family had a lovely birthday breakfast at home. Then, later in the afternoon, they went for lunch at one of my favourite Chinese restaurants.

17

In fact, I was the one who called to make the reservations. And even though I wasn't there, I could smell the food miles away. I was sad I couldn't join them.

That day, not only did I miss out on my mother's birthday celebrations, I also got into a fight with my sister. I was miserable. Nothing seemed to be working out for me.

Next was my niece's one-year birthday party. My sister had put a lot of effort into planning this party and I knew it was going to be a blast. Although I wasn't quite sure if I was still invited, I looked forward to attending. We had even sewn special Indian outfits for the party. I wasn't going to miss it for anything in the world – unless of course that thing was actually a human being growing inside of me.

My mother burst my party bubble and told me emphatically that I was not needed at the party. Bedrest was bedrest and so I would stay at home while the rest of the family enjoyed themselves at the birthday party. How mean?! Humph!

A day after the party, one of my younger cousins came to stay with us. She needed a place to stay urgently and I couldn't turn my back on her. Although I hadn't planned on having family come to live with us so soon, her arrival was timely because I really needed help around the house. She helped with cooking and cleaning. More importantly, it was comforting to have some company during the day when my husband was at work.

After spending four weeks at home, I began to feel impatient. Christmas was fast approaching, and I didn't want to miss out on all the fun. Christmas is a festive season with numerous exciting events and a special time for Yaw and me. Since we first met, we had always had fun-packed Christmas celebrations, so it was ironic that now that we were finally married, our first Christmas was to be spent indoors with no chilling. I tried hard to be positive and focus on the joys of becoming a mother, but it wasn't always easy. And seeing pictures of my friends having fun without me didn't help either. By this time, I felt out of the loop in our circle of friends. I felt as if I was out of touch with everyone. The initial excitement my friends had about my pregnancy seemed to have fizzled out quickly, and since I was stuck at home on bedrest, I was left out of the fun. I was secretly upset with them because I felt that they were not trying hard enough to reach out to me while I was at home. But I knew that I couldn't stop them from having fun.

Back at home, I looked forward to Christmas Day. Our first as a married couple. Although I would have loved to prepare a fancy Christmas meal, I simply didn't have the strength to do that. But I still planned to make Christmas Day special for us.

On Christmas morning, I got up, started getting dressed up, and was almost ready for church when I decided to call my parents to wish them a "Merry

Christmas." When I told my mother I was getting ready for church, she was surprised. "You don't seem to understand what it means to be on bed rest," she said. My mum was a professional midwife, so I knew I had to listen to her advice. Besides, it was better to err on the side of caution because the life of my baby was too precious for me to take risks. With that, my plans of attending church service on Christmas morning were flung to the same place my party aspirations had gone – out of the window. I spent Christmas morning at home watching church service on TV.

For lunch, I put together some of the leftover meals from the food my mum had sent me during the week. Not exactly the fancy Christmas meal I would have liked. Yet, we had a lot for which to be thankful. It was our first Christmas as a married couple, and we had a baby on the way.

Since I wasn't allowed to go to church on Christmas Day, I knew Watchnight Service on New Year's Eve was out of the question. I love to dance. And I was fully aware that my dance moves alone were enough to send the baby out on its way. So, I stayed at home with my cousin, and we watched the service on TV. I must admit that it wasn't the same as being in church, but I knew that it was for a good cause. After all, my new mantra was "Baby first".

Still, December of 2011 would go down in the books as the most boring Christmas of all time! I looked forward to the New Year and prayed that it would bring me excitement and wonderful blessings.

Chapter Five

JANUARY 2012 – NEW YEAR'S DAY

Unfortunately, January did not start off as well as I had anticipated. I had imagined that my husband and I would stay at home together and share our hopes and aspirations for the year ahead. Sadly, I realized, he had other plans. He and a few of his guy friends had planned a trip to the beach. That meant I would spend the day at home alone. And if there's anything worse than being stuck at home, it is being stuck at home alone. I felt sorry for myself. How I wished I could also go to the beach! I was angry with my husband for leaving me at home and going to hang out with his friends. In fact, I wasn't just angry, I resented him for this. Why did I have to be the only one making sacrifices for our baby? It wasn't fair!

As I wallowed in self-pity, I tried not to think about all the fun that my husband was having with his friends. I wished he would call to check up on me. I didn't want to call him, because I didn't want to appear too clingy.

Around 6 pm, he was still not back from the beach. At that point, I lost it! I couldn't hold back the tears any longer, so I had a full-blown pity party for myself. I was so upset that I decided to go for a walk up the hill to vent out my frustrations. In hindsight, that wasn't a very wise decision for someone on bed rest. Yet, I needed to get out of the house to clear my mind. So off I went up the hill. On the climb up, I came across a group of little children who were having the time of their lives racing up and down the hill barefoot. Their joy was so contagious that I managed to pause my pity party long enough to laugh with them.

As I walked back home, I prayed that my husband would be back from the beach. I had missed him terribly. Yet, I didn't want to make it so obvious that I missed him. I was also hurt because I felt abandoned. How was I going to communicate that to him? So many thoughts ran through my mind as I neared the house. Lo and behold, when I got to the gate, his friend's car was parked outside. The boys were back!

I couldn't control my feelings. But instead of telling him how I felt, I sulked the whole evening. Somehow, he seemed oblivious to my unhappiness, and that made me even more miserable. The more oblivious he seemed, the more I sulked. After an hour or so, I had had enough! I needed to take my silent protest up a notch. So what did I do? I decided to leave the house to go and sit outside on the front porch in pitch darkness and in the midst of a choir of mosquitoes. I was hoping he would come and look for me and lovingly hold my hand and take me back inside the house. But that didn't happen.

Instead, he called out my name through the window, as he looked around the house for me. I responded and told him I was outside. After waiting for a few minutes for him to come outside and take me back into the house, I realized that wasn't going to happen. So I had no choice but to drag myself back inside all by myself.

Once inside the house, I finally mustered courage and told him that I had had such a miserable day at home while he was out having fun with his friends. He looked confused. He then told me that he didn't have fun either. Apparently, he had a lot on his mind too and so had gone to the beach to help him clear his head.

He had a lot on his mind. Expecting a baby was no joke! We were both worn out. We had our fears, yet we didn't know how to express them. I could only imagine how he felt. Because he didn't have a bump, he didn't get any sympathy or expressions of concern. But I could bet that his mind was exploding with a list of all the things he had to put in place before our child was born. He was working full-time as well as pursuing an evening MBA programme. And he was doing all this in addition to adjusting to life as a newly married man and expecting a baby in a few months. Whew! That was a lot for anyone to handle.

I realized how unreasonable I had been. I had spent

the whole day sulking just because I thought he was having more fun than I was. In the end, I apologized to him because my cold reception had also hurt him. No one wants to come home to an unhappy wife. I felt bad, and I hoped that his friends hadn't caught any of my 'sulking' vibes.

While I wished that I had been more understanding, I was still disappointed that I didn't get to spend New Year's Day with my husband.

As if being stuck at home wasn't bad enough, I had a dental accident too. As my husband was getting ready for the beach in the morning, I was eating my favourite Shortbread biscuit while watching Bishop T.D Jakes preach on TV. All of a sudden, I felt a hard pebble-like substance in my mouth. I was shocked because I had never seen anything like that in Shortbread biscuit. Perhaps, it was an imitation brand and not the original McVities? I wondered. However, when I looked at the 'pebble' I realized it did not come from imitation Shortbread. The pebble was part of my tooth that had broken off. How weird!

I rushed to the bathroom to examine my mouth and see exactly where I had lost part of a tooth. I was bleeding a little, but it was nothing to worry about. I couldn't believe that my tooth had chipped off just like that. Without any warning. I hadn't felt any pain or discomfort prior to the 'accident'. It just came off. Maybe I was chewing too hard on the Shortbread.

Maybe.

When I told my husband, he was just as weirded out as I was. We laughed about it and decided that I needed to see a dentist ASAP. The thought of going to the dentist freaked me out! I am petrified of seeing the dentist. Since I had my tooth extracted at the age of 12, I have avoided going to the dentist. I wasn't looking forward to the return trip. But with the gaping hole in my dentition, I didn't have to think twice about that decision.

Chapter Six

ANTENATAL CLINIC II

During my bedrest, my only chance to see the outside world was when we went for antenatal clinic appointments at the hospital. January held the promise of an end to my 'solitary confinement' a.k.a. house arrest. I eagerly anticipated our next antenatal clinic appointment. Besides getting an update on the development of our Baby, any reason to get out of the house was welcome news. At the hospital, the doctor did an ultra sound scan, took some measurements of the Baby – length of limbs, etc. and declared that I was fit to resume work and other social activities. Yippee!!! We survived the first trimester!!!

Interestingly, the doctor also informed us that we were now going to start with the "antenatal clinic proper". Apparently, the first three months had basically been a trial period, and we were now going to be given our antenatal booklet. Also, the fee for antenatal consultation was lower than the special consultation fee that we paid during the first three months. Antenatal consultation also came along with routine lab tests and ultrasound scans. It was serious business. In effect, we had graduated to the maternity class. Hurray!!!

I looked forward to antenatal clinic appointments. On those days, I put in extra effort to look nice. I didn't want to be the frumpy-looking pregnant woman at the hospital. I also selected an outfit that would give the doctor easy access to my growing bump. A blouse and skirt/trousers combo was ideal because that way, I only had to pull the blouse up and push the skirt/trousers down. Wearing a dress was tricky because I would have to lift the dress aaaaallllll the way up to show my bump, and that was just too revealing.

Once we arrived at the hospital, we would go through the same routine. First up, retrieve my folder. Next, take my vital signs – temperature, blood pressure, and weight. For some reason, the nurses never told me what they recorded. It seemed that that information was reserved for the doctor. But I was curious, so I always asked them whether it was within the normal range. Knowing my vital signs was important to me. Well, except for my weight. Not that! While on the scale, I would close my eyes so I don't see the numbers. I didn't want to know what the nurses recorded. See, I had never weighed so much in my life! And when the scales hit 80kg during my ninth month – yes, I peeked – I was alarmed! How was that possible? I never imagined that I could weigh so much! So, although my doctor assured me my weight gain throughout pregnancy had been stable and normal, I still harboured doubts. I wondered why I wasn't like some women who hardly gained any weight during pregnancy.

Another unpleasant part of antenatal clinic was the lab tests. I didn't realize I would need so many during pregnancy. But all the lab tests were necessary. They checked sugar level, infections, and a host of other conditions that could potentially endanger my, and the baby's, life if not detected early enough. For example, the fasting blood sugar test could detect gestational diabetes, and for this lab test, I had to eat my last meal by 7 pm the previous day. The first time I had to do this test, I made sure my husband and I arrived at the hospital early because I was starving! I even took along a snack to dive into right after the test. But to my dismay, when we got to the hospital, the lab technician had not yet arrived. Unbelievable!

We asked the receptionist to call him to find out how close he was to the hospital. A few minutes later, she explained to us that he was running late. 10 minutes…20 minutes…30 … and still no lab technician. I was furious. Didn't he know he was dealing with a pregnant woman whose appetite had quadrupled? "I would definitely tell him my piece of my mind," I thought. Yet, when he finally showed up, I was so relieved to see him that I forgot to scold him for keeping me waiting. I wanted him to finish with the test as soon as possible so I could eat.

My favourite part of antenatal clinic was the actual consultation with the doctor. This was mainly because he usually performed an ultra sound scan, which was almost like getting to meet my Baby. I looked forward to the ultrasound scans because they assured me that my Baby was developing well. I also got to hear the Baby's heartbeat. It was incredible! Let me admit something here, though. Most of the time, I couldn't see whatever it was that the doctor and my husband pointed to on the screen. Everything looked black and grey. "Hands? Where?" I would be confused. Yet, simply knowing my Baby was safe and sound – that was enough for me.

Antenatal clinic appointments were fun, but they were also incredibly expensive. Since I didn't have any proper health insurance, I had to pay out of pocket for every single visit. Consultation, lab tests, scans all added up to a significant amount. Although it was worth every pesewa spent, it would have been nice to have it all covered by health insurance.

Chapter Seven

MATERNITY WEAR

After I had been cleared to resume work, I faced another challenge. I was about four months pregnant by then and though I was still wearing my pre-pregnancy clothes, they had become rather snug around the waistline. I could squeeze into my jeans, but closing the button was an impossible task. Clearly, it was time to start shopping for maternity clothes

That was when I realized that I couldn't find ANY decent shops that sold maternity wear in Accra. On my computer, I had a folder of trendy maternity clothes from various stores in the UK, but I couldn't find anything similar in Ghana. Where did pregnant women shop? I wondered. I thought of going to Accra Central, Ghana's central business district, to look around the shops. But I just couldn't muster the time or energy to make that trip.

I was also on the lookout for shoes. My feet appeared to have expanded along with my bump. Shoes I managed to squeeze my feet into had become too uncomfortable to walk in. So, along with new clothes, I needed to buy new shoes. I didn't realize being pregnant would be so expensive! Fortunately, I got some decent shoes in a second-hand shop at Haatso, so I didn't have to break the bank for new shoes.

Shopping for a whole new wardrobe was frustrating! Especially so because just before I got married, I had a new set of office wear, which I never got the chance to fully outdoor; and here I was, having to put together yet another brand-new wardrobe.

I am not a fan of the 'typical' Ghana maternity look – a gathered dress with a high waist – but options to buy what I preferred were few. My last resort was to have them made by a seamstress. Fortunately, one of my friends is a seamstress so I entrusted my maternity wardrobe to her. She did her best and made some beautiful outfits for me. But nothing quite matched the pretty dresses I had seen online. Still, I was determined to slay throughout my pregnancy, so I made do with the few clothes that I had.

Chapter Eight

PREGNANCY VIGILANTES

It wasn't until I resumed work and other social activities that I realized that being on bedrest had shielded me from the pregnancy vigilantes who take great delight in commenting on all pregnancy-related issues and giving unsolicited advice. Perhaps, because this was my first pregnancy, they thought it necessary to teach me how to take better care of myself and the Baby. It was even more annoying when these 'experts' were mere acquaintances. Yet, no topic was off-limits to them. Weight gain. Eating habits. Choice of hospital. Preferred sex of baby. The list was endless....

So soon?

Some of the pregnancy vigilantes were not very happy with the fact that we had wasted no time in getting pregnant. I remember one family friend engaged me in a long discussion about how it would have been better to enjoy my marriage first before having children. I thought to myself, "Well, if children are so bad for marriage, why have them at all?" Besides, at that point, what good was that advice?

What exactly did she want me to do? Terminate the pregnancy so I could enjoy my marriage?

Others also 'jokingly' hinted that we had spared no time in conceiving. These types of comments were more embarrassing than annoying, particularly when they came from older people. Were we expected to practise abstinence although we were married? I was confused. Ironically, these same people would have been equally concerned if we had waited too long before getting pregnant. It was simply impossible to please everyone.

But the most annoying ones were those who claimed that, by their own calculation of my cycle, I had gotten pregnant before the wedding. These people gave me coy smiles and silly looks as if to say that they knew my secret. Seriously?

Boy or Girl?

The pregnancy vigilantes also needed to know whether I was having a boy or girl. Perhaps, it was so they could get a customized present made for the Baby. All the same, I found such questions not only intrusive, but also aggravating. What difference did the sex of the baby make?

Apparently, it meant a lot, because people had different theories of which sex was better to have as a first-born child. While some thought it was good to 'give' my husband a boy first, others thought a baby girl would make him happier.

There was also the group of super experts who could tell the sex of the Baby just by looking at my bump. If the bump was very big then it was a boy. Also, if I was having a difficult pregnancy then it was a boy. The problem though, was that some of these indicators were conflicting. For example, some people also swore that difficult pregnancies were associated with baby girls. I found these predictions amusing, so I kept quiet and simply played along with the experts.

Abrewa

The first time someone called me "Abrewa" (Old Lady), I was confused. I was in church wearing what I thought was a pretty yellow dress. "Who? Me? Abrewa?" I thought she was referring to the style of my dress. Sadly, I soon learned that 'Abrewa' is a term used to refer to pregnant women in Ghana. How mean!

I hated that nickname but was stuck with it for nine long months.

Some people took delight in deflating my self-esteem, by shouting "Abrewa" whenever they saw me. It didn't matter if I was in church or out on a date; they had decided that "Abrewa" was a much more appropriate name for me than my given name "Awura Amma". I cringed each time someone called me 'Abrewa'. I could never get used to that name.

Obolo

The vigilantes were also weight watchers. Once my bump began to show, I received mixed reviews on my weight. While some people commended me for "keeping my figure", others cautioned me to "check my weight". Although my doctor had assured me that my weight was within the normal healthy range, some of the vigilantes disagreed and didn't waste any time in telling me I was getting fat. I did not understand why they were so concerned about my weight.

One afternoon, while I was cooking at home, a relative who was visiting whispered in my ear that as soon as the baby is born, I should make it top priority to lose all the pregnancy weight. That comment came as a complete surprise. I had been working very hard that day and thought she was going to tell me to get some rest. Instead, she indirectly called me fat.

Another time, while I was drinking black tea at the office, an elderly colleague walked in and sternly instructed me to stop drinking my tea. She had assumed that the tea was loaded with sugar and milk, so she went on to give me a lecture on how I needed to watch my diet so that I didn't gain too much weight. She went on and on about how getting fat would lead to a caesarean section, which would then make it difficult for me to bond with my child. She had her own theory that women who gave birth via caesarean section did not have motherly love for their children. Unbelievable!

Again, during an Easter barbecue, one of my sister's friends directed me to put down the khebab I had just picked up. Apparently, eating the khebab would make me gain weight, and that would make my Baby so big that he would have to be born through caesarean section. A caesarean section was terrible because it would make it impossible for me to lose the belly flab, and that would obviously be the end of my fabulous life.

It appeared that I had been put on a strict diet without my consent. I wanted to scream to all the people who commented on my weight gain, "Leave me alone! Of course, I have gained weight. There's a tiny person growing inside me!"

Free tip to all the weight superintendents: if you care so much about a pregnant woman's weight, why don't you do something more productive like offering to be an exercise buddy or paying for full-membership at a plush fitness centre? Now THAT is being part of the solution.

Chapter Nine

FEBRUARY 2012 – HALFWAY THERE!

Boy or Girl?!

Somehow, from the moment I found out I was pregnant, I referred to the Baby as a boy. I just had a strong feeling that I was carrying a boy. I couldn't rationalize that feeling to my husband, but I trusted my instincts. Surprisingly, he was indifferent about the sex of the baby. He was excited to have a baby and that was all that mattered.

We looked forward to confirming the sex of our Baby. I felt that once the sex was confirmed, the fact that we were going to have a baby would become even more real. We could even start thinking of names and begin shopping for him.

We had to wait until the fourth month to find out the sex of the Baby. It was around this time that the genitals had developed well enough for the sex to be identified. Although I was confident that I was having a boy, it was still exciting to wait for the doctor's confirmation (or otherwise). After moving the probe around my belly during the ultrasound scan, he announced it, "It's a boy!" We were excited! I was happy that my intuition had been proven right. I already shared a special bond with my son.

20-week scan

Shortly after the gender reveal, the doctor asked us to go to an advanced diagnostic centre for a detailed scan. He explained that this was routine procedure carried out at the 20-week mark to check that the Baby was developing normally. Among other things, the scan would look out for cleft lip, chambers of the heart, limb formation and other physical features.

I was extremely nervous. The radiologist wasn't as friendly as our doctor. She was busy taking measurements and making notes of whatever she was seeing in the scan. We had to probe before she opened up to share what she was recording. When she wanted to examine our Baby's face, he was in a position that hid his face. After several attempts, she decided to move on to examine his limbs. Just when she was about to let me go, I asked her to check again for the position of the Baby. Perhaps, he had changed his position and his face could be examined. To my pleasant surprise, I was right! When the radiologist checked, he had moved his position again. I was pleased to hear that his facial features were intact and that he did not have a cleft palate.

We were so pleased with the results of the ultrasound scan that we went for a photo shoot right afterward. We had to document the day.

Shopping

Now that we knew the sex of our Baby and knew he was healthy, it was time to start getting ready for his arrival. I browsed several websites to help me compile a list of all the items we needed to buy for our son. Surprisingly, after window shopping in several shops in Ghana, I realized that things were much more expensive in Ghana than they were in the UK. So I decided to shop online instead.

I couldn't believe the tall list of things that I 'needed' for our son. Did I really need everything on the list? I tried to categorize the list into "Must-have" and "Nice-to-have", but the "Must-have" list was longer than anticipated. Apart from selecting colours and patterns, I also had to guess the size of our son at birth. Will he fit into the new-born size? Or will he move straight to size 0-3 months? With limited funds, I had to be sure that everything that I purchased would be of use.

I love lists. So, with the help of several websites, I put together a checklist as well as a shopping list.

Activity Schedule

February 2012

- Kegel exercises
- Start planning for nursery school
- Schedule standard mid-pregnancy ultrasound
- Start shopping for maternity clothes
- Sign up for child birth classes
- Plan a babymoon
- Put together a first aid kit
- Sewing kit
- Order cot
- Paint nursery

March 2012

- Send money to Jasmine to buy stuff
- Consider taking maternity photos
- Start interviewing paediatricians
- Revisit money and legal matters
- Schedule a glucose tolerance test
- Take a tour of your maternity ward
- Pamper yourself
- Start preparing nursery
- Ship baby's stuff from UK

April 2012

- Talk to your doctor about what to expect during labour/delivery
- Others feel baby move
- Start taking fetal counts
- Start babyproofing your home
- Interview carers and/or day care centres
- Braxton Hicks contractions
- Buy baby's crib and mattress
- Buy baby's clothes and essentials

May 2012

- Learn the signs of preterm labour
- Get an easy-to-maintain hairstyle
- Cook and freeze meals for after delivery
- Get any items still needed for baby
- Install car seat
- Research on circumcision
- Buy diaper bag and stock up on essentials
- Buy a high chair
- Attend childbirth class

June 2012

- Get to know the signs of labour
- Last week to fly safely
- Pack hospital bag
- Last day of work

- Finalize maternity leave paperwork and plans
- Schedule non-stress test
- Schedule a biophysical profile
- Start washing baby clothes
- Research vaccines
- Prepare yourself for labour and delivery

Wow! Some of these items are rather 'extra'. It would have been helpful to have a website that was suited for the Ghanaian environment. It would certainly have eased the anxiety a bit.

Shopping List

Baby

[ ] 4-8 undershirts or vests (snaps at neck or wide head openings, snaps under crotch)
[ ] 4-8 one-piece pajamas
[ ] 1-3 rompers or other dress-up outfits
[ ] 4-7 socks or booties (shoes are unnecessary until baby walks)
[ ] 1-3 hats (broad-brimmed for summer baby, soft cap that covers ears for winter baby)
[ ] Crib, cradle or bassinet
  - Slats no more than 2 3/8 inches apart
  - Corner posts no more than 1/16 of an inch above frame
  - No cutouts in headboard or footboard
  - Top rails at least 26 inches above mattress

[ ] Firm, flat mattress fit snugly in crib (less than two
    fingers should fit between mattress and crib)
[ ] 2-4 fitted crib sheets
[ ] 4-6 soft, light receiving blankets
[ ] Changing table or cushioned changing pad for
    low dresser or bureau, with safety strap or railing
[ ] Changing table pad
[ ] Diaper cream
[ ] Unscented baby wipes (causes less irritation)
[ ] Soft washcloths
[ ] 6-10 dozen cloth diapers and 6-8 diaper covers,
    or 2-3 large boxes of disposable newborn-size
    diapers
[ ] Baby soap
[ ] 10-16 bottles and teats both four and eight ounces
    (if fed strictly by the bottle, baby will go through
    about ten in the four-ounce size per day)
[ ] Burp cloths (or cloth diapers)
[ ] Formula (if not nursing)
[ ] Pump (if you plan to breast feed)
[ ] Milk storage bags (if you plan to breastfeed)
[ ] Baby nail clippers or blunt scissors
[ ] Baby thermometer
[ ] Petroleum jelly and sterile gauze (for circumcision
    care)
[ ] Infant or convertible car seat

Nursery

[ ] 1-2 heavier blankets (for colder climates)
[ ] Rocking or arm chair
[ ] Music box, sound machine or CD player
[ ] Crib mobile with black and white images (remove
      when baby can support self on hands and knees)
[ ] Baby monitor
[ ] Nightlight
[ ] Dresser
[ ] Toy basket
[ ] Swing or bouncy chair

Feeding

[ ] 10-16 bottles and teats, both four and eight ounces
     (if fed strictly by the bottle, baby will go through
     about ten in the four-ounce size per day)
[ ] Bottle warmer (cuts down on nighttime trips to
      and from the kitchen)
[ ] Bottle sterilizer (if your dishwasher doesn't have
      one)
[ ] Bottle brush
[ ] Dishwasher basket for small items
[ ] 4-8 bibs
[ ] Burp cloths (or cloth diapers)
[ ] High chair
[ ] 2-4 pacifiers
[ ] Formula (if not nursing)

For nursing moms

[ ] 1-3 nursing bras (Breasts swell following birth, so
      start with one size larger than your maternity bra.
      Wait until size settles down – about two weeks
      after birth – to purchase additional bras.)
[ ] Nursing pads
[ ] Nipple cream
[ ] Nursing pillow
[ ] Pump (even if you plan only to nurse, a pump
      will allow you to leave milk for baby if you want
      or need to separate)
[ ] Milk storage bags

Hospital Bag

[ ] Insurance info, hospital forms and birth plan (if
      you have one)
[ ] a pair of slippers
[ ] A warm robe or sweater you don't mind sacrificing
      to the cause
[ ] 2 maternity bras -- no underwire -- and nursing
      pads (whether or not you plan to nurse, you'll
      appreciate the support and leak-protection)
[ ] Lip balm (hospitals are very dry)
[ ] Toiletries and personal items -- hairbrush,
      toothbrush, toothpaste, deodorant, face wash,
      makeup (as if), shampoo, conditioner, lotion,
      contact lens case and solution (remember,
      travel-sized products are your friends)
[ ] Headband or ponytail holder (avoid clips -- they'll
      probably poke you)

[ ] Sugar-free hard candy or lozenges to keep your mouth moist during labor (candy with sugar will make you thirsty)

[ ] Pen and paper

[ ] Non-perishable snacks (you'll probably be hungry after labor, and the hospital cafeteria could be closed)

[ ] Cell phone and charger, phone numbers of people to call after birth, prepaid calling card (if your hospital doesn't allow cell phones)

[ ] Camera, film or extra memory card, battery or charger

[ ] A gym bag packed with a change of clothes and basic hygiene products for your partner

Take it or leave it

[ ] Extra pillow (with a case that can get ruined, in a pattern distinguishable from hospital white)

[ ] Comfortable going-home clothes in six-month maternity size and flat shoes (or, just wear the clothes you came in… sorry, but they'll probably still fit)

[ ] Bath towel

[ ] Your favorite brand of soap, shampoo and heavy flow sanitary pads (the hospital supplies these things, but bring your own if you're picky)

[ ] A few pairs of maternity underwear that can get ruined (the hospital will have disposable pairs, which some women find handy and others find gross)

[ ] A ruin-able nightgown (you can use those lovely
    hospital gowns, but your own might help you feel
    more human)
[ ] Very light reading (think mags and newspapers,
    not War and Peace)
[ ] Your MP3 (loaded with your favorite tunes, of
    course)

Leave Home

[ ] Any clothes or nighties you really like (they will
    get ruined)
[ ] Stopwatch (your nurse or a monitor will take care
    of timing contractions)

What to Bring For Baby

[ ] Approved car seat
[ ] A coming-home outfit
[ ] Warm blankets (for the ride home)
[ ] Outdoor gear like a snowsuit and hat, as
    seasonally appropriate (remember, babies are
    extra sensitive to cold)

Nursery

A few things to keep in mind as you put together
baby's nursery:

[ ] Finish all painting and wallpapering at least eight
    weeks before baby is expected, and leave windows

open for aeration until the actual arrival. These activities release potentially harmful fumes, but finishing them early should eliminate any risk to baby.

[ ] Notice where light enters the room. Don't put the crib somewhere that receives direct sunlight in the morning or is under a streetlight all night.
[ ] Check that none of the crib slats are more than two and 3/8 inches apart, and that all the bolts and screws are tight. Make sure there are no gaps between the mattress and crib, and look out for any small parts or plastic coverings.
[ ] Keep comforters and pillows out of the crib -- they could suffocate baby. If a pretty blanket came with the crib set, try hanging it on the wall or using it on the rocking chair.
[ ] Make sure there's room to replace the crib with a bed once baby is ready.
[ ] Use wood or cork floor or area rugs rather than wall-to-wall carpet if you can. They're all easier to clean, and don't harbor as much allergy-inducing dust.
[ ] Secure rugs to the floor with double-side tape. Wouldn't want one to slip while baby's in your arms!
[ ] Figure out how much storage space you'll need… then put in more. Almost without fail, parents underestimate the amount of stuff they'll acquire.

[ ] Don't forget somewhere for you to sit, and make it comfy. You'll spend lots of time reading and

rocking in that chair.
[ ] Keep all diaper supplies close to the changing
    table, so you don't have to move far from baby to
    reach anything.
[ ] Place furniture away from the windows, and use
    window guards. Also, cut off any blind or curtain
    cords, or put them up out of reach.
[ ] Anchor all heavy furniture to the wall so it won't
    fall over if accidentally bumped.

Whew! What a tall list! No wonder I was
overwhelmed at the sheer magnitude of all the tasks
that I had to complete before our son was born.

PREGNANCY HIGHS AND LOWS

Pregnancy was a rollercoaster. Sometimes, I was extremely happy to know I was going to be a mother. Other times, the physiological changes were so overwhelming that I wished I could fast forward time to delivery day. Pregnancy is no joke! Until you have experienced it, you cannot even pretend to imagine what it feels like to carry a baby inside you. And even after you have experienced pregnancy, you cannot claim to be an expert because every pregnancy is different.

Fortunately, pregnancy was not always a bad experience for me. Pregnancy came with perks that I thoroughly enjoyed.

Highs

Bust

One of the first signs of pregnancy was my enhanced bust. Usually, I am barely a B cup. But once I got pregnant, my cup size steadily increased to a C cup and I loved it!

Glow

Pregnancy glow exists, and it is glorious! I experienced this the most during the first trimester. When I put pictures up on Facebook, people commented on how radiant I looked. I enjoyed receiving those compliments. They were a much-needed boost for my self-esteem.

Special treatment

I also enjoyed the special treatment I received. While it is true that pregnancy is not a disease, there are enough discomforts associated with pregnancy that a dose of special treatment every now and then is welcome.

In general, people were more willing to give me a helping hand by assisting me with seemingly heavy loads, offering their seats, and allowing me to jump the queue. At home, expectations fell significantly, and I wasn't under pressure to cook and clean. I knew that my health was top priority, so I didn't do anything that stressed me out. It was nice to be able to relax and take it easy.

But pregnancy was not always enjoyable. There were also some...

Lows

Puffy Face

The pregnancy glow soon gave way to a puffy face. For some reason, all my facial features – nose, cheeks, and lips – were swollen. No matter how hard I tried to disguise the puffiness with make-up, it still wouldn't go away. I became self-conscious and I wasn't particularly fond of taking pictures anymore. I didn't even look like myself. I looked like someone else.

Heartburn

My second trimester came with sleepless nights. First culprit: Heartburn. It was worse when I ate spicy foods and foods containing tomatoes. Unfortunately for me, most of my favourite foods are either spicy or made with tomatoes, or BOTH! That meant no shitor and no gravy – my food options dwindled significantly. But I don't give up easily, so sometimes I was stubborn and would eat those foods anyway. Then, later at night when it felt as though the heartburn had literally set my heart on fire, I would regret it. My poor husband! He just couldn't understand why I tortured myself this way.

Sleeping position

Apparently, the best sleeping position for a pregnant

woman is on her left side. Although I have doubts about this theory, once I had been advised to sleep on my left side, I had to comply because I didn't want to risk harming my Baby. But sleeping on one side only was near-impossible because I am not one to stay in the same position during the night. No! I like to toss and turn!

When I was about 11 years old, my family and I went to our hometown, Bonwire, for my auntie's customary marriage. When we got there, there weren't enough beds for each of us, so I shared a bed with the Lady Reverend Minister we were travelling with. The next morning, she was distraught! Apparently, I had kicked her the whole night, tossing and turning in bed. But I couldn't remember a thing. I had slept soundly and had no idea of the torture she had endured.

So, you see, making a sudden shift from sleeping in various contours and angles, to sleeping on only my left side for nine months was a huge sacrifice. After a few months, I got bored with the view from the left, so I switched things around and moved my pillow to the tail of the bed. However, this meant my husband and I were sleeping in a weird head-to-feet position. But it worked for me - it was refreshing to have a different view for a change. I couldn't wait for our Baby to be born, so I could go back to my tossing and turning.

P is for Pee

I didn't realize that pregnancy would make me pee a gazillion times a day! As my pregnancy progressed, so did the urge to pee. Seriously, it felt like I had to pee ALL the time! Along with the incessant pee came the realization that there is an acute shortage of decent public restrooms in Accra. And even when they are available, they are often hidden in obscure corners with no directional signs. This often meant having to ask for directions. Really? Did I need to make a public announcement of my need to empty my bladder? How about a simple sign pointing to the restroom? Was that too much to ask for? Sometimes I would go back and forth in my head trying to decide whether to announce my desire to pee by asking for the restroom, or whether I could make it back to my office or home in time without peeing on myself. Such needless torment! When I was lucky enough to find a restroom, eight out of ten times, it was a mess, making me wish I hadn't gone there in the first place.

As if heartburn and sleeping on one side were not enough to prevent me from sleeping soundly, I also had to get out of bed several times to pee. Once I woke up to pee, it would take another half hour or so for me to get back to sleep. Only to have to pee shortly again after that! Sigh!

Chapter Eleven

HE'S HERE!

By the eighth month, we were ready to meet our little man. His room was ready. His clothes had been neatly folded in his closet. We were ready to welcome our new family member. One of my favourite moments of getting ready for our son was when my husband assembled the cot. He beamed with pride as he screwed different parts together. He was excited to be a father, and I knew he would be a great one.

As the due date got closer, I began to feel anxious. I wondered what the experience would be like. When would labour start? Where would I be? Would I be close to the hospital? Where would my husband be? How would it feel? There were so many uncertainties, and a thousand-and-one questions ran through my mind. Since I didn't know when and where I would go into labour, I carried my hospital bag in the boot of my car everywhere I went. I didn't want to be taken by surprise.

Packing the hospital bag was no easy task. I had to pack clothing and other basics for me, my husband

and our son. While I didn't want to pack our entire closet, I also didn't want to leave out any essentials. After packing and unpacking several times, the final result was a bulging medium-sized hospital bag. I was quite pleased with myself.

Now that our hospital bag was ready, I eagerly waited for my Baby to show his face. I had even selected the perfect day for him to make his appearance. Although his official due-date was 2nd July 2012, I wanted him to be born on 28th June 2012. The reason for my choice was simple. I love the number six, so I wanted him to be born in June, the sixth month. I also wanted him to be born on a Thursday just like his father. The last Thursday in June fell on 28th June 2012. And it was close enough to the due date that he wouldn't be premature. It seemed like a frivolous wish, but I prayed to God to grant me my request.

As the day approached, I wondered if my dream would come true. I had read about the first signs of labour and activities that could trigger labour. A common sign that labour is near is the breaking of the woman's 'water' (This is when the amniotic sac bursts and the amniotic fluid comes out.) I was worried about where my water would break. Would it happen while I was out in public? How much water should I expect? Would it be a sudden gush like a broken water pipe? Or would it be a gentle trickle? I even considered carrying an extra set of clothes just in case my water broke while I was away from home.

Unfortunately, the breaking of water isn't a guarantee that labour will start the next minute. In fact, for some women, labour could still be days away, while for others, labour may start even before their water breaks. So, contrary to popular belief, it wasn't the most reliable indicator of labour.

Another sign that labour is on the way is a light bleeding called 'the show'. But just like the breaking of water, this is also not 100 percent foolproof. For some women, after the show, labour could still be days or even weeks away. For others, labour could set in a few hours later. So, I eagerly awaited the breaking of my water, or the show, or BOTH!

On Tuesday, June 26, I felt some cramping in my abdomen. I wasn't sure if I was having contractions, but it didn't really matter then, because it was the wrong day. So, I prayed very hard that it would stop. And thankfully it did.

On Wednesday, June 27, I felt just fine. No cramps. No contractions. Nothing. That wasn't good either. If I was going to have my son the following day, then at the very least I should have started feeling some contractions. I should feel him getting ready to make his way out.

To be honest, I didn't even know what I was feeling anymore. If I felt a contraction, I second-guessed myself. Was it just my imagination? Was that a real contraction? I almost didn't know anymore. So, when

I began to feel 'contractions' around 2 am on Thursday, June 28, I didn't wake my husband up. I wanted to wait it out to be sure that it wasn't just my mind playing games with me. I started timing the contractions and they were about 10 minutes apart. That was a good sign, but I still didn't say anything because I didn't want to raise a false alarm. In fact, I wasn't even sure if I was actually feeling the contractions or just imagining them.

About half an hour later, I went to the bathroom to pee and there it was, THE SHOW!!! Finally, a sign that labour was near. On a Thursday too! I was cautiously excited! Cautious, because I knew that it could still take days before the onset of true labour. Yet, it seemed very likely that our son would be born on Thursday June 28, 2012. I was overjoyed!

Labour

I woke my husband up and told him about the contractions and the show. I was excited! After nine months of waiting, we were finally going to meet our little boy. We called our doctor, and he asked us to wait 'till sunrise, and then head to the hospital. So, we got ready and set off for the hospital.

When we left home around 5:30 am, the contractions were already getting close in succession, and a bit painful too. It was the most uncomfortable car ride ever. With each pothole and speed ramp, the pain level increased. I couldn't stay seated as I had suddenly developed waist pains. I just wanted to lie down and relax.

During a stop at a filling station mart, I could hardly sit through the contractions. I wanted to yell at my husband to hurry. I needed to get to the hospital as quickly as possible. Finally, after what seemed like an hour, he returned to the car with some snacks, and we continued our journey to the hospital.

When we got there, we were taken to a private ward to wait for the doctor on night duty. After an extremely painful and uncomfortable examination, the doctor informed us that, although I was only 3 cm dilated, my cervix was softening – a sure sign that our Baby was truly on his way. I couldn't believe that I was only 3cm dilated. Surely, I had progressed more than that! The contractions were very painful, and to think that the level of pain could triple terrified me. I couldn't even imagine how painful the contractions would be when I was 10 cm dilated.

Shortly after the first physical examination, the anaesthesiologist came by to inquire if I was interested in an epidural. He reminded me that the pain was going to get much worse, so opting for an epidural would help to manage the pain. Although I wanted to scream, "YES!", I had decided weeks earlier not to get an epidural. There were several side effects of getting an epidural and I didn't want to take any chances.

Waiting…

Now that labour had been confirmed, all we had to do was to wait until our Baby was finally ready to show his face. A few hours after we arrived at the hospital, my mother joined us with a basketful of breakfast goodies. We ate together and continued to wait.

In the meantime, my mother sent for items to spruce up our hospital room. She got a lovely basket, napkins and a nice cloth to cover the lockers. She wanted the room to be perfect for her grandson.

Lunchtime came by and there was still no real progress. We ordered some Chinese food for a pre-delivery celebration. After lunch, my big brother, Josh, also joined us as we waited for our son/grandson/nephew. We talked and laughed to pass the time. All the while, my husband was busy recording the contractions on his iPad. He was my personal midwife.

Finally, at about 1 o'clock in the afternoon, my Doctor arrived, and I was glad to see a familiar face. During what I thought was a repeat of the physical examination done earlier that morning, I was stunned when he literally turned my uterus inside out. He explained that he had performed a membrane sweep, to speed up the pace of labour. The membrane sweep appeared to be successful as the contractions became more frequent (and more painful too). I couldn't lie down anymore, so I paced up and down the room. To manage the pain, I breathed through the contractions, just as my mother had taught me. I knew it wasn't time to cry yet. I was saving my energy for pushing.

About three hours later, the doctor came by again. Still not satisfied with my progress, he decided to move me to the labour ward. Our son had to come out. Since persuasion had failed, force was about to be applied! Once in the labour ward, the doctor broke my water in a very uncomfortable procedure, pushing what looked like a plastic cane, wayyyyy up my uterus until water gushed out. All was not well though. The water was green. It was stained with meconium (baby poop) and that was not good. It was a sign that the Baby was in distress. Labour had taken too long and the Baby, too, was getting tired. We needed to get him out fast!

I was also given an oxytocin infusion to speed things up. I was happy because I knew oxytocin worked like magic and would speed up labour. What I didn't realize was that it would also quadruple the intensity of the contractions. Shortly after I received the infusion, excruciating pain spread through my waist and lower back. Sitting on the bed was impossible. Lying down was uncomfortable. Although I was given a dose of pethidine to alleviate the pain, it had absolutely no effect whatsoever. Soon after the pethidine shot, I threw up all the food I had eaten. It wasn't a pretty sight. The pain was unbelievable. I struggled to hold back the tears. I didn't want to talk and laugh anymore. In fact, I didn't want anyone to see me in so much pain. I wanted to be alone.

Suddenly, I felt the urge to use the washroom. It was too strong to be ignored. The nurse advised me not to go. She feared that it was the Baby on his way out, and she didn't want me to give birth in the toilet bowl. But at that point, I didn't care. All I knew was that I needed to get to the washroom immediately. Once I got there, it felt incredibly nice to sit on the hollow seat. I was happy to have some relief from the pain – albeit temporarily.

After a while, it became obvious that the oxytocin infusion, too, had failed to help our Baby out. Since he couldn't come out by himself, the only option left was to have the doctor take him out. It was time for a caesarean section.

This was not how I had envisaged my birth experience. I didn't expect that getting my Baby out would be such a long and tedious process. What happened to my birth plan? I thought only fat babies had to be born through caesarean sections? I thought only women with severe pregnancy complications had to have caesarean sections? I was disappointed. I couldn't hold back the tears anymore. I felt I had let everyone down, but my husband and mother reassured me that it wasn't my fault. Some things were simply out of my control. I didn't have to blame myself for not being able to have a 'normal' delivery.

The caesarean section was necessary to ensure the safe delivery of our Baby.

There was no time for an emotional meltdown. I had read about foetal distress and I knew that we were in a medical emergency, so I composed myself and got ready for the surgery. Ironically, just when I put myself together, I was told that the theatre was not yet ready for me. Apparently, there had been a caesarean section earlier that afternoon and the room was still being set up for the next patient, who happened to be me.

I wasn't sure if the nurses fully understood what was at stake. My Baby had to be born within the shortest possible time! It was an emergency, and they needed to act fast! I wasn't going to lose my Baby or jeopardise his health just because a nurse was arranging surgical instruments on a silver tray. The pain, coupled with the fear of potentially harming our Baby, made us furious. We couldn't waste any more time, so my mother asked my husband to wheel me to the theatre. If they weren't going to come for me, I would go to them. Although the medical team was not pleased when we showed up at the door of the theatre, that was the least of our worries. We needed them to treat the surgery with the urgency it deserved.

A nurse reluctantly wheeled me inside and asked me to sit on the operation bed. While the anaesthesiologist gave me a shot in my spine, he casually asked me questions about the tattoo on my lower back. It seemed that they had been through so many emergencies that they had lost the adrenaline rush to act quickly. After receiving the spinal, I was asked to lie on my back. As I lay there, I heard the anaesthesiologist and the doctor arguing over whether to let my mother come into the theatre. While the anaesthesiologist felt she should not be allowed inside, the doctor insisted that she be allowed to enter. In the end, the doctor won. I was happy to have both my husband and my mother at my side. I knew I was in safe hands.

The anaesthesia only affected my lower body, so I was still able to see and hear all that was going on in the theatre, except for the surgery itself. A screen had been put up across my mid-section, so I couldn't see what the doctor was doing. Although I didn't feel any pain, it felt like the doctor was tugging at my insides. After a while, I started to doze off, but tried hard to stay awake. I had waited nine long months to meet my little boy, and I didn't want to miss a thing. I prayed that the doctor would be quick. I couldn't possibly be asleep when my son was born.

He's Here

Finally, my Baby was taken out. He was here. What a miracle!

Yet, it felt like I was dreaming. It was as if I was in someone else's body. I could not immediately make the connection that he was mine. It was surreal. I couldn't believe I was a mother. I wondered how it would feel to hold him in my arms. I couldn't wait to hold him. I couldn't wait to see what he looked like. I had to be patient though, as he needed to be cleaned up first. Meanwhile, the doctor stitched me back up in a very very very long process.

Finally, after what seemed like an hour, the doctor was done, and I was wheeled back to our private ward where a large welcome party – made up of grandparents, grandaunts, aunties, cousins, and close friends – was anxiously waiting to welcome our new-born. Everyone was delighted and thanked God for the safe delivery of our son.

After about half an hour of praying, praising God and taking pictures, the welcome party was dispersed to enable us to get some rest. Since we had a double occupancy room, my husband stayed with us at the hospital. Having him there with us was extremely helpful. When the Baby woke up during the night, he would carry him out of the cot and lay him by my side for breastfeeding. Although many men are uncomfortable with handling a new-born, my husband was a natural. Right from the theatre, he held our son in his arms and carried him to our room. The bond between father and son was remarkable. While we were at the hospital, his favourite sleeping position was being rolled up into a ball on his daddy's chest. He was already daddy's boy.

Chapter Twelve

HOSPITAL STAY

Our private ward was quite nice. There were two beds, two side lockers, a television and an en-suite bathroom. The hospital staff were also incredibly helpful. There was Daniel, the male nurse who took care of me from the moment I checked in at the hospital up until the day we were discharged. He had been on night duty when I first reported on Thursday morning, but my doctor had asked him to stay on to assist with the delivery. Daniel was a wonderful nurse. He made me feel comfortable and at ease. When he was around, I knew I was in safe hands. He knew his job and it showed.

There was also the female nurse, Nafisa, who took care of me the morning after. She was very understanding and assured me that I was going to be okay. That morning, she came by before 6 to assist me to bath. She explained each procedure to me and made me feel comfortable. I was grateful to have kind nurses taking care of me.

We enjoyed VIP treatment while we were at the hospital. In the mornings, the Otoos, our family friends who lived nearby, would bring us a basketful of breakfast goodies – tea, toast, eggs, sausage, you name it! It was breakfast fit for royalty. Then for lunch and supper, between my mother and my mother-in-law, we always had more than enough to eat. We were truly grateful for all the love and care that we received.

We were also overwhelmed by the love and support that people showed us in the first few days after our son was born. Friends and family came by the hospital to visit us and to see our son. My mum ensured that we took pictures with all those who came by. So now, we have a picture story of our stay at the hospital. Although we were thrilled to have people come over, by Saturday afternoon we were exhausted. We longed for an afternoon nap, but we couldn't ignore our guests who had gone out of their way to visit us.

Taking Baby Home

On Saturday, two days after delivery, the doctor was pleased with my recovery, and informed us that we would be discharged on Sunday. We were delighted! We couldn't wait to go home to our own space.

It turned out that the hospital bag that I had been so proud of wasn't quite adequate. I had left out a few essentials, so during our short stay at the facility, my husband went back home to get those items that I hadn't packed – a bucket, more clothes, pillows, and cover cloths among others. So, by Sunday, our luggage had doubled. It was as though we had been away for a whole month!

On Sunday, we woke up early in the morning and packed our bags ready to go. But first, we had to wait for the doctor to officially discharge me. We also had to wait for my mother, who had offered to give us a ride home. By early afternoon, after the doctor had officially checked us out, it was time to go home.

When my mum arrived, she was surprised to see me in a blue and peach outfit. Apparently, in Ghana, in the days, weeks and even months following childbirth, a mother is expected to wear white as a sign of victory and celebration. And there I was, without a single item of white clothing. She immediately took off her white pearl bracelet and put it on my wrist, promising to get me some white clothes as soon as possible.

Leaving the hospital was quite a spectacle as my mother insisted that we take pictures to document this epic event. We took pictures in the ward, in front of the ward, at the reception, in front of the hospital, and in front of the car. We took pictures with phones, with iPads and cameras. We took pictures posed and unaware. We didn't joke around with the pictures. As we left the hospital, she reminded us that we were blessed to be leaving with our baby. Having lost her twin boys in May 1985, she knew too well the pain of leaving the hospital without a child. So, we sang and praised God for the miracle of a safe delivery.

At home, Grandma Beatrix (Baby Yaw's paternal grandmother) and the rest of the family were anxiously waiting for us. It was emotional as she thanked God for bringing laughter to the home again. Barely two years before Baby Yaw was born, that same living room was filled with tears and sorrow as we paid our last respects to Grandpa Prempeh (Baby Yaw's paternal grandfather). Indeed, "weeping may endure for a night, but joy comes in the morning" (Psalm 30:5). Baby Yaw's birth signified a new dawn in the family and we were grateful to God.

Chapter Thirteen

HOME WITH BABY

Now that we were back at home, the reality of motherhood began to set in. I knew motherhood would have its fair share of challenges, but I was optimistic that I would be a fast learner and would quickly adjust to my new role as a mother.

Soup Diet

In Ghana, it is common practice for new mothers to have lots of soup to enable them produce enough breast milk. So, while I was still on admission, my mother-in-law made sure that I always had soup. When I arrived home, I wasn't surprised to see a fridge stocked with all kinds of soup - groundnut soup, light soup and palm nut soup. She had been very busy cooking up a storm while we were in hospital. Bless her!

Baby Blues

The first few days at home were difficult. Motherhood wasn't what I had envisioned. I had expected an automatic transition to a motherhood state of mind, but that didn't happen. It hadn't yet sunk in that I was a mother. When I looked at my son, I didn't make an immediate connection that he was mine. I wanted to be a mother. I was glad that I was a mother. I loved my son with all my heart. Yet, somehow, I didn't feel the euphoria that I often associated with motherhood.

I wondered if there was more to motherhood. I longed to feel that warm rush of excitement that I had always imagined. What made matters worse was that I didn't know how to communicate those feelings to anyone. I didn't want to create the impression that I was ungrateful and self-centred. Far from that! I was immensely thankful to God for my son. I just didn't know what else to do.

I had imagined that my days would be filled with laughter and merry making. I assumed that family and close friends would come by to spend time doting on our handsome son. I didn't realize that the birth of our son was not the beginning of a vacation for everyone. People had other things to do. It wasn't all about me and my baby.

Lonely

Instead of getting used to my new role as a mum, it seemed my challenges were increasing by the day. I felt as if no one really cared about me anymore. All the attention was on Baby Yaw. He was a fragile new-born so understandably people were more concerned about him. But I also mattered. In fact, I was having a much harder time than he was. He didn't have any cares in the world. I was the one who, although still recovering from surgery, took care of his every need. Taking care of a new-born was not easy! I had to feed him (constantly), burp him, change his diaper, and make sure he was comfortable. Yet, I was lost in the shadows as everyone fussed over Baby Yaw. Perhaps, they assumed that, just like all other mothers, I would be fine. Eventually.

The day after we took our baby home was a public holiday, so everyone was around to help out. Fast forward to the next day and I was at home alone with Baby Yaw. How did that happen? Well, my husband had to go back to work. He was eligible for only two weeks of annual leave and we were saving that for his final examination period in December. With no paternal leave, he had no option than to go back to work. My mother-in-law also had duties in her family business that she needed to attend to, so she had to go to work. Unfortunately, earlier that morning, the nanny called to inform us that due to a family 'emergency', she wouldn't be able to come to work. I wanted to be strong, so I lied that I would be fine. I told everyone that they could go on with their normal business because I was going to manage just fine. So, there I was at home, all alone with my five-day old baby. I was distraught.

Fortunately, after speaking to me over the phone, my mum could sense the sadness in my voice. So, she asked our family friend - turned – sister, Comfort and my driver-turned-brother, Thomas, to come over to keep me company. I can't tell you how happy I was to see them. It was a huge relief to have someone else watch Baby Yaw for just a few minutes, so I could grab something to eat or use the washroom, or just to rest

One-Week Old

On our son's one-week birthday, my parents surprised us with a visit to celebrate with us. Their visit meant a lot to me because they lived quite a distance away from us, and it would take them at least two hours to get back home. Yet, they wanted to be with us because among the Akans, a child's one-week birthday is very significant. In fact, a child is not even considered a human being until he survives the one-week milestone. So, the one-week birthday is a celebration during which parents and other family members thank God for the gift of a new baby. Together, my husband, parents, mother-in-law and our marriage counsellor, sang hymns to praise God for giving us a baby boy, and for keeping him safe. I am thankful for parents who make time for celebrations.

Circumcision – The 'Necessary' Evil?

Unfortunately, the celebration was short-lived as the very next day, we took Baby Yaw to the hospital to be circumcised. For some reason, I had assumed that the doctor would perform the procedure himself, and that would have been my preference. But he assured me that he would let an experienced nurse from one of the teaching hospitals perform the procedure. He explained that there was a new method in which a ring was tied around the baby's 'willy' and left there until the foreskin fell off with it. It sounded very simple and painless, so I didn't give it much thought.

We arrived at the hospital on time to meet the nurse. However, to our disappointment, she was late! The worst part of waiting was that each time we called her, she would lie that she was only 15 minutes away. 15 minutes became 30 minutes, then one hour. Finally, after almost three hours, she arrived at the hospital. Since the painkillers had worn off by then, Baby Yaw was given another dose, and then he was taken to the treatment room for the procedure. My husband went along with them, but I opted out.

When they hadn't come out after 30 minutes, I started to get worried. "Why was it taking so long?" I wondered. Then I heard Baby Yaw cry out in pain. What had we done to our baby? I felt terrible. I hadn't expected him to cry. I thought it would be painless. But I was wrong - he screamed and shouted for about ten minutes, and then thankfully, the pain medication knocked him out and he fell asleep even before we left the hospital. I heaved a sigh of relief. As long as he wasn't crying, I was fine. Happy baby, happy mummy .

When we got home, I took him to the bedroom for a diaper change, but I was terrified by what I saw: my Baby's willy was pink and swollen. It had been tied with a string, and it looked extremely painful and uncomfortable. That was definitely not how I had imagined the procedure would turn out. I ran out to call the nanny and asked her to continue with the diaper change. I couldn't stand seeing my son in so much pain. Why did a new-born baby have to go through this painful experience? And to think that this was the supposedly less painful option?

Recovering from surgery

In the midst of the baby blues, circumcision, and other frustrations, I was still recovering from my surgery. The morning after my caesarean section, I felt surprisingly strong. I even walked up and down the hallway at the hospital to the amazement of my mother who explained that 20 years ago after undergoing a caesarean section a woman would be stuck in bed for at least a few days before she could even walk. Yet there I was walking and moving about as if nothing had happened.

When I was discharged from the hospital I was given some painkillers and antibiotics. I was simply discharged with no guidelines on how to care for myself to ensure a full recovery. I didn't know what to expect during my recovery. What could I do safely? Which activities did I need to stay away from? Nothing.

A week after childbirth, I began to feel some pain at the site of incision. Initially, I ignored it, but as it intensified, I knew that something was wrong. Some friends and family dismissed it as "normal" surgery discomfort. But there was nothing normal about the pain I felt. It worsened whenever I had to bend to pick up Baby Yaw from his cot - and I did that a lot!

So, during my two-week post-natal review, I talked to my doctor about the pain and he explained that it was most likely caused by the separation of the skin during the surgery. He assured me that it would go away in no time. Sadly, the pain rather increased. It was so bad that it kept me awake all night. The last straw was when one night I developed a fever and was literally shivering in my bed, while my abdomen was burning in pain. Something was definitely wrong!

The next day, my mum picked me up and took me back to the hospital. When the doctor examined me, he noticed that there was a swelling above the incision, so he injected it to see if it was filled with any fluid. Although there wasn't any fluid in the swelling, he went on to poke several places so that if there was any fluid, it would flow out easily. I also had a lab test and the results showed that I had caught some form of infection. So, I was given some more antibiotics and painkillers and sent off on my way.

The following morning, I noticed some liquid coming out of the places where the Doctor had injected the previous day. So off I went back to the hospital. My sweet mother had to leave work again to pick me up to the hospital- God bless her! Although my doctor wasn't on duty, he asked my favourite nurse, Daniel, to attend to me. In a very painful procedure, he drew up all the liquid from the swelling. The pain was so unbearable that he had to stop midway to give me a shot of pethidine. The procedure took some time, as he wanted to ensure that everything was drawn out. My mum requested that they take a sample of the liquid to the lab to identify exactly what type of infection I had caught.

A few weeks later, the lab results revealed that I had caught a staphylococcus infection, and my doctor explained that it was most likely caused by using a weak concentration of methylated spirit while I was on admission at the hospital.

I was furious! I had suffered so much just because someone hadn't cared enough to dilute the methylated spirit solution properly. I had gone through excruciating pain and sleepless nights. I had been to the hospital no less than five times in one month. How was I supposed to rest when I was continuously moving in and out of the hospital? The worst part of it all was that I had paid for every single visit for them to treat me for an infection that THEY had given me in the first place. I wanted to have a word with the hospital administrator. At the very least, I wanted an apology for making me go through needless pain. I even thought of taking legal action against the hospital. But I simply didn't have the strength and the resources to take them to court. Besides, I really liked my doctor, and I didn't want him to be implicated because of someone else's negligence.

So, without anyone taking responsibility for the pain I had been through, I had a full-blown pity party for me, myself and I. I felt sorry for myself. Why were things not going according to plan? Why did I have to have a caesarean section? Why did I get an infection? Why did I have to go through so much pain? It seemed unfair that while some women went through childbirth unscathed, I ended up with a host of complications.

Colic

Despite the initial challenges of adjusting to motherhood, I was grateful to God that we had a happy baby. While we were still on admission at the hospital, the nurses praised him for being calm. His calmness was even more apparent because a baby girl who was born a few hours before him was the exact opposite. She did not just cry, she wailed, and she shrieked. She cried so loudly that we heard her from across the hall. In fact, when she was upset, the whole maternity wing of the hospital knew it. We felt terribly sorry for her mother. Surely, it would be depressing for your baby to cry so much just hours after birth. We were happy with our calm baby. Even when he cried, it wasn't a piercing shriek. It was more of a whimper.

Then one day, when he was just about two weeks old, he started to cry – a loud, inconsolable, never-ending cry. Nothing could make him stop. Nothing. Sometimes he would pause for a few minutes. But just before I heaved a sigh of relief, he would start crying again. It was extremely frustrating because we didn't know what was making him cry and we didn't know how to make him stop.

After this went on for a few days, we did some research, and realized that it was colic. It usually started around 4:00 pm (soon after the nanny had left – hmmmph!) and would go on for as long as two hours. Although we learned that colic wasn't harmful to our baby, that didn't make it any easier to cope. Sometimes, he would bend over as if he was in pain. Other times, he would stretch out his arms while crying. I was convinced that there was something wrong with him. Why would he cry for hours if he was perfectly fine?

My poor hubby! After a tiring day at work, he was welcomed home with a bout of colic. How depressing! Yet, as soon as he arrived home, I wanted him to take over, so I could also take a break from unsuccessfully trying to soothe Baby Yaw.

We tried all the remedies we had read about – gripe water, burping after every feed, rubbing his back - but nothing seemed to work. The crying could get so bad that I would also break down into tears. None of my nieces had had colic so this was completely new to me. I never thought that I would have to deal with anything as distressing as colic.

It took a lot of inner strength to wait for him to calm down by himself. Sometimes, it felt like all my strength had evaporated. Thankfully, we were not alone. We could call on family for support. My mother-in-law would often rock him in her arms to try and soothe him. My parents were also very supportive and kept on assuring me that Baby Yaw would be fine. One evening, when he was about three weeks old, the colic was so bad that my parents had to leave a wedding reception to come to my rescue. When they arrived, I was exasperated and in tears. I was at my wits' end!

One Saturday, the colic set in earlier than usual. I was home alone with my cousin when Baby Yaw started to cry. No amount of rocking, singing and cooing would soothe him. He simply refused to calm down. I took him outside for fresh air to see if that would work. I was exhausted! What had I done to deserve this? I was miserable. As I sat on the wall of our porch with a crying baby in my arms, I actually considered throwing him over the wall. I was losing my mind. I called my husband and asked him to come home immediately! I couldn't deal with the colic all by myself.

During our six-week consultation with the paediatrician we told him about the colic, and like everyone else, he told us that it was normal. He explained that colic causes parents more pain than the babies. He was also sceptical about the supposed remedies for colic. He said all we had to do was to stay calm and loving throughout the crying. "Easier said than done", I thought to myself. Then, as if to show the doctor what colic could be like, Baby Yaw started to cry and shriek. The doctor felt sorry for us. He said, "That's very colicky", and went on to reassure us that it would soon be over. I didn't believe him though. It would take divine intervention for this extreme colic to end. All I wanted was a happy baby. Was that too much to ask for?

When we got home that evening, we braced ourselves for yet another bout of colic, but to our surprise, he didn't cry. Not even a whimper. Nothing.

"Could this be it?" "Was this the end that the doctor had promised?" I didn't want to get my hopes up. I didn't even want to jinx it by talking about it with my husband. We both thought about it, but we were too scared to talk about it. The next day, we wondered if he would start to cry again, but to our (pleasant) surprise, he didn't cry that day or the day after that or the day after that or the day after that. The colic was gone forever! Hallelujah!

Naming Ceremony

According to Akan custom, we should have performed the naming ceremony a week after our son was born, but we scheduled it for his one-month birthday to allow me to fully recover from surgery, and to allow Baby Yaw to adjust to his new environment.

Since he had been born on a Thursday, he was automatically called "Yaw". So, he had a name even before the official 'naming' ceremony was held. However, that was not enough. We also needed to determine who he would be named after. Among the Akans, it is the responsibility and privilege of the father and his family to give the child a name. So, I left the choice of name entirely to my husband. I knew that it meant a lot to him, and I wanted to give him that honour of choosing a name for our son.

He had two options. Since our son had been born on Thursday, just like him (my husband), it was natural to name him after himself (Yaw Sarpong Agyeman-Prempeh Jnr). In fact, some people had already started calling our son "Junior". But my husband wanted to honour his late father, Mr Kofi

Agyeman-Prempeh, so he decided to name our son after him. That way, our son had a bit of both his father and grandfather. He shared a day name with his father, and he was named after his paternal grandfather. Lucky boy!

We had both the naming ceremony and the baptism at our church. Having the two ceremonies together was significant. Through the naming ceremony, our son gained an identity. He was named after his paternal grandfather, so he was called Yaw Agyeman-Prempeh. The family name indicated that he belonged to a wider community of people, and through the baptism, he was dedicated to God. The Reverend Minister explained that baptism signified that our son belonged to God and God alone. Thus, no matter what he did or where he went, since he had been dedicated to God, God would always bring him back to the right path. How reassuring!

Although his official name was Yaw Agyeman-Prempeh, somehow, we had already started calling him Nana Yaw, so that became his nickname.

The naming ceremony was scheduled for 6:30 in the morning, so it was a mad rush at home to get ready. Thankfully, we made it to the church on time. I prayed that Nana Yaw would be on his best behaviour during the service. God answered my prayer and he slept throughout the service. He was fast asleep. Even when the Reverend Minister poured water on his head during the baptism, he stayed asleep. I couldn't believe my luck.

I was overwhelmed by the expression of love from our family and friends who managed to make it to the church very early on a Saturday morning. After the short service, we went outside for pictures – lots of pictures! We then went back home to continue with the celebrations. First, we served breakfast, then lunch, and even an early dinner. I was touched – I hadn't expected so many people to come by. I thought it was just a simple naming and baptism ceremony, but our family and friends surprised us. It turned out to be an all-day celebration.

Chapter Fourteen

LIQUID GOLD

Breastfeeding

Even before my son was born, I knew that I would breastfeed him. After all, breast milk, also known as liquid gold, is touted as the best source of nutrition for babies. I looked forward to that special mother-child bond that I had heard so much about.

Breastfeeding was indeed a remarkable experience. It was special. I loved to see the look of satisfaction on my son's face as he suckled at the breast. But that's not the whole story. Breastfeeding was also extremely challenging. In fact, I was surprised at how difficult breastfeeding could be. You see, because of the tiny size of babies' stomachs, they can only have a little milk at a time. So instead of having three meals a day like most adults do, babies need to feed about five to seven times during the day, and in my son's case four to six times during the night as well. Whoa! Breastfeeding was a full-time job.

Despite the difficulties involved in having to breast-feed day and night, I tried to make the experience as special as possible. My mother had told me that it was important for me to look at my son and smile at him while breastfeeding. So, in the mornings, after my husband and my mother-in-law had left for work, I would sit in a chair alone with Baby Yaw and sing to him while I nursed him. My favourite hymns were:

My God Loves Me
My God loves me
His love will never end
He rests within my heart
For my God loves me

His gentle hand
He stretches over me
Though storm clouds threaten the day
He will set me free

My God loves me
His faithful love endures
And I will rest like a child
Held in love secure

Sometimes I would choke while singing the second verse. It was amazing how this hymn reflected my situation at that point in time. Although I was struggling as a new mother, I was comforted by the knowledge that God was in control in spite of the difficulties I was experiencing.

Another favourite is a Presbyterian Hymn of praise:

Dɛn na menfa menyi w'ayɛ
Tumi wura daasebrɛ
Fa wohonhom pa no ma me
Na masɛm ayɛ wo fɛ
Na wo dɔ nsɛnkyerɛne
Ne wo dom no
Tra m'adwene
Tumfo ne Ohen kɛse
Yɛ dawase yi w'ayɛ

I enjoyed this morning routine immensely. It was my morning devotion with Nana Yaw and I cherished it. However, as the hours went by and the fatigue increased, I could no longer sing and look lovingly in his eyes while nursing him. In fact, sometimes I would nurse him while fighting back tears, wondering when motherhood would get easier for me.

Initially, I had planned to feed my baby exclusively with breast milk for the first three months, and then transition to formula. I even had feeding bottles and SMA ready for the transition. So, you can imagine my shock when I found out that the recommended period for exclusive breastfeeding was six months and not three months. It didn't make sense to me. My maternity leave was only three months, yet I was expected to breastfeed for six months? It simply didn't add up.

Six months was a looooonnnnggg period. That was half a year. How come I had never heard of that? I wasn't prepared for such an 'extended' period of breastfeeding. I didn't think I could do it. I didn't even want to do it. But I felt I had no choice. I had to put my baby's needs first, so I continued to breast-feed him for three more months.

By the time Nana Yaw was four months old, his appetite had quadrupled, and breastfeeding no longer helped me lose weight. Instead, it sapped my energy and made me hungry all the time. Sometimes, after breastfeeding several times during the night, I would be so hungry that I would have to get out of bed and grab a quick snack in the middle of the night. I was on the fast lane to weight gain.

Breastfeeding was intense! It was a 24-hour job. There was no break. Remember when I thought I was having sleepless nights during pregnancy? Well, that was just the beginning of the end of a good night's sleep. The first few weeks after our son's birth, I began to long for the nights of heartburn and discomfort. Nothing could have prepared me for the sleepless nights that came with breastfeeding my son. It was unbelievable.

A typical night involved having to wake up to breast-feed barely two hours after I had put him down to sleep. After feeding him, I would rub his back to help him burp. By then, he would have pooped, so I would change his diaper before putting him back in his cot, only for him to wake up after about an hour and a half to repeat the cycle. This could go on about four to six times each night. It was sheer torture. I was miserable. I couldn't understand why my baby had to wake up so many times during the night.

House Arrest

Before Nana Yaw was born, I used to describe myself as a 'home girl'- I wasn't overly fond of going out, especially to crowded places. My idea of a perfect evening was relaxing at home with a good storybook or a good movie. So, when my mother advised that I stay at home with my son as much as possible for the first three months to protect him from infections and to keep both of us well-rested, I didn't think it would be difficult. "Easy enough" I thought to myself. "I will spend my time bonding with my baby and staring lovingly at his handsome face. Why would I want to go out when I had such an adorable baby at home?"

Boy, was I wrong! After a few weeks, I realised that taking care of a new-born wasn't very exciting. In fact, most of the time, it was plain boring. His days were characterised by sleeping and feeding. When he wasn't doing any of these, he would just stare into space. I had imagined that he would immediately start cooing and babbling, so the silence was killing me. I was bored. I wondered if he even knew who I was. I needed some more excitement in my life.

In fact, I yearned for some adult interaction. Sometimes, I longed for a few minutes by myself away from home. Unfortunately, since I had decided earlier not to express my milk (because of the erratic power supply), I couldn't go anywhere without my son. We were like Siamese twins joined at my breast – we went everywhere together! But I needed some space to catch my breath and to reconnect with the outside world. I missed date nights with my husband. Friends didn't bother to invite me out anymore. I feared my days of enjoying adult company were over. I felt trapped. I realised then that I wasn't a 'home girl' after all.

Are We There Yet?

The challenges of breastfeeding took me by surprise. I wasn't prepared for the sleep deprivation and constant fatigue. I thought that since breastfeeding was the natural way of nourishing babies, it would be easy. Little did I know that it could also drive me insane. Several times, I almost gave up, but my husband always managed to convince me to make it to the sixth month mark. "Do it for Nana Yaw", he would say. Somehow, he made me laugh with his pleas. I couldn't wait for his six-month birthday. The countdown was on.

I took it for granted that once Baby Yaw turned six months, he would automatically transition to formula. I assumed that after six long months of exclusive breastfeeding, he would thank me for nourishing him with my breast milk, give me a pat on the back for all the hard work, and merrily move on to explore formula and other foods.

To my horror and dismay, that did not happen. The first time we attempted to feed him formula from a bottle, he simply spat it out. A few times, he swallowed a little and suddenly changed his mind and spat the rest out. It was extremely frustrating and disappointing. The transition to formula did not happen at this time. Although he began to eat cereal, pureed fruits, and other forms of solid food, he continued to vehemently reject formula. His loyalty was to breast milk, and he wasn't going to move on so quickly. I was crushed. Since, he still needed milk, I had no option than to continue breastfeeding him.

Chapter Fifteen

EMOTIONAL ROLLER COASTER

When I was pregnant, I knew that all the hormonal changes I was going through could make me emotional. I would be happy one moment and be in tears the next. The least thing triggered such strong emotions that it felt like I was on a roller coaster. But that was normal for a pregnant woman. I assumed that after childbirth, my hormones would zap back to their normal levels, and I would have more control of my emotions. But I was in for a surprise. As a new mother, I was an emotional wreck. A combination of fatigue, sleep deprivation and anxiety kept my emotions in 'roller coaster mode'. Sometimes, I even surprised myself at how volatile I could be.

I was happy to be a mother. I had looked forward to having a child, and my dream had come true. I knew I was blessed to have a son so soon after getting married. Nana Yaw was adorable. He had a head full of hair, and he looked just like his daddy. It felt good to know that together, my husband and I had created such a handsome little man. I loved my new title of "mother". I was among the first within my circle of friends to have a child, so I had bragging rights there. It's hard to explain, but being a mother gave me a sense of accomplishment. I didn't care if I wasn't the richest person, or the most beautiful person. I was a mother, and that was a big deal. Call it vanity, but I was a proud mum.

It wasn't always pure joy, though. Sometimes I was disappointed at how motherhood had turned out for me. Nothing seemed to be working as I had planned. I was tired most of the time. I didn't have enough help with childcare. I was stuck at home. I didn't have any time for myself. My friends were too busy with their own lives to visit. There was a lot of drama going on in my own family. This was definitely not how I had envisaged life as a new mother. I felt let down. I didn't deserve all these difficulties! What had I done wrong?

I was in need. I love being independent and in control. I don't like being in need, so I try as much as possible to do things on my own. But once I became a mother, I realized that I couldn't do everything on my own. I needed help, but it was difficult for me to ask for help. I expected people to know what I needed. So, when they didn't see my need, I felt dejected. It was as though they were deliberately ignoring my needs. "Couldn't they see that I was tired?", "Didn't they know that I was hungry?", "Couldn't they tell that I needed a break?" Nobody seemed to know what I needed.

I also resented the fact that I seemed to be the only one whose life had changed drastically. I never thought of how motherhood would change my life. In fact, I assumed that after I gave birth, I would simply go back to doing things the way I had always done them. But I realized that my life had changed, and I couldn't go out as I pleased. Yet, my husband seemed to be going about his normal daily routine. I resented it. It was unfair that I was the only who was making sacrifices for our son. I also wanted to be able to go out and have fun. I just wanted to be free. No strings attached.

Once, when my husband had to travel to Kumasi for a friend's wedding, I was upset the whole night. I hadn't been feeling well that day and I longed for a break. I was feeling dizzy and I could barely stand on my feet. I wished he would stay with me that week-end and help with childcare. I resented him for being able to take a trip to Kumasi. I felt cheated. It was unfair. I wanted to enjoy that same level of freedom. When he left for the airport, I broke down into tears. I was miserable.

I resented the assumption that I was the primary care giver. Everyone else simply 'helped' out when it was convenient for them. But for me, I had no choice. I was responsible for Baby Yaw. Period. This was probably one of the most difficult issues that I had to deal with as a new mother. I needed a break. I wanted to be able to take a nap without being woken up to breastfeed my son. I wanted to attend social events and also have fun. I wanted to watch a movie uninterrupted while someone took care of my son. I hated it when the first option to soothing our son when he started crying was to take him to his mother – me! I even suspected that some people intentionally pinched him for him to cry just so they could give him back to me.

I was a wreck. My emotions had spiralled out of control.

I felt abandoned by my husband. I was overwhelmed with breastfeeding and sleepless nights, and I wished he would do more to help out. I knew his hands were full as he was working full-time and pursuing a Master's Degree alongside. Yet, I wanted him to do more. I felt as though his life was going on while my own life had been turned upside down. So, whenever he did anything outside work and school, I got upset. I wanted him to rush home as soon as he closed from work or school. And when he got home, I expected him to take over with childcare immediately. He was a parent too and I wanted him to have a feel of what I went through during the day. I knew he wanted to spend time with us too. But at that time, I didn't care about his intentions.

Chapter Sixteen

RAISING A HEALTHY BABY

Immunisation

Like circumcision, immunisation shots are a necessary evil. In primary school, we learnt that there were six childhood killer diseases that babies needed to be immunised against: Tuberculosis, Diphtheria, Whooping Cough, Tetanus, Measles and Polio.

The day after Baby Yaw was born, my husband and my mum sent him to the child welfare clinic for his Bacille Calmette-Guerin (BCG) shot. I was surprised when they had to take him to another centre for that immunisation. I had assumed that vaccinations were done at the individual hospitals, but I was told that not all hospitals are immunisation centres. I expected them to be gone for a while, so I was worried about having to breastfeed Baby Yaw. Surprisingly, they were back in no time. They explained that, as an incentive to get them involved, fathers did not have to join the queue. What a relief!

The BCG immunisation didn't have any adverse

effect on Baby Yaw, so we were happy. In fact, by the time they got back to the ward, he had stopped crying. It was as if nothing had happened to him. He was a strong boy. This was the beginning of a series of immunisations. At his first visit, he was given a book with a schedule of immunisations that he needed to take. His next immunisation was in six weeks' time, and we looked forward to that. For convenience, we transferred his file to a hospital which was just ten minutes away from our home. My husband enjoyed taking him to the Child Welfare Clinic, and I felt so blessed to see the look of satisfaction on his face each time we took our son for weighing and/or immunisations. Of course, most of the time, he was the only father there, and the nurses were full of praises for him.

At the week 6 appointment, we were shocked when we found out that he was going to receive not one, not two, but THREE immunisations all at once. One shot on each thigh, and an oral one. That was just too much!

Apparently, a lot had changed since my primary school days. Instead of six childhood killer diseases, there were now about 10 of them!!!!! Poor Baby Yaw! I couldn't bear the sight of him being injected so I stood outside while my husband held him. I felt terrible when he cried out in pain. It was torture!

The nurse told us to give him paracetamol syrup three times a day. She also informed us that he might get a high temperature, so if that happened we were to tepid sponge him. We also had to put some ice on his thighs to prevent them from getting swollen. Whoa! This was just too much. I didn't realize that immunizations could be so complicated. I felt sorry for my little baby.

That night, we could hardly sleep. His temperature shot up and I was very scared. You see, just two days before Nana Yaw was born, my little niece suffered a convulsion and it was very frightening. One moment, her temperature was 37°C, the next moment, she was convulsing. With this in mind, I knew that high temperature in children needed urgent attention. I didn't want to fall asleep - I wanted to monitor his temperature throughout the night. I gave him paracetamol whenever I felt his temperature rising. I also called our family doctor a few times just to be sure that it was alright to manage the fever at home. He assured me that 37°C was within the 'normal' range, so there was no cause for alarm. But I needed to tepid sponge him to stop the temperature from rising any further. All this while, our baby was still fast asleep. When we put the tepid water on his feet, he started to cry. He was very upset. I was in a fix! I knew he needed to be sponged, but I also couldn't bear to see him so upset. I remember that as a child I also hated being sponged, so I sympathised with him. But I had to be a good mum and do what was best for him.

After the tepid sponging, his temperature dropped to

36°C and we put him back in his cot. A few hours later, when we checked his temperature, he had become very hot again, so we had to repeat the procedure. No one told me that immunisation was so much work! Fortunately, by the next morning, his temperature had stabilised and there was no more sponging.

I dreaded the week 10 appointment with all my heart! I was right. It was just as bad as the week 6 appointment.

By then, I didn't even want to think about our week 14 appointment. I considered skipping it, but I knew no school would admit him if his immunisation record was incomplete, so I was compelled to take him through another ordeal. Besides, my husband would not even hear of skipping an immunisation. So, I psyched myself up for another night of tepid sponging. But miraculously, there was no fever! Perhaps his body had gotten used to the vaccines by then. He had become a pro. Thankfully, that was the last time he had to receive three vaccinations at a go.

Home Nurse

As a mother, I always pray for good health for my baby. But with my overactive imagination, the slightest sign of ill health would quickly develop into a tragic disease in my mind.

Fever

I detest fevers with all my heart. They are truly the bane of a child's health. A fever could signal anything and everything. It could be nothing more than a cold, and it could be as serious as meningitis. So, I didn't take any chances. The moment my son's temperature went above 37°C, I would call our family doctor for guidance. I didn't want to take anything for granted. I would rather over-react and cover all bases, than take things for granted and jeopardize my son's health. I soon became a professional at tepid sponging- starting from the feet and slowly working upwards to the head.

Cold

"What is the best way to clear a baby's blocked nose?" This question doesn't seem relevant until you have a four-month old baby with a blocked nose. I used to take my ability to blow my nose for granted, until I realized that babies simply don't have the energy and the technique to blow their own noses. So, something as simple as a blocked nose can cause a great deal of discomfort.

A cold often meant sleepless nights for both baby and mummy. Usually, when he had a cold, he also got a fever, and that caused me a lot of anxiety. I always thought about the worst-case scenario. What if it was bronchitis? Or pneumonia? Or some other serious chest infection?

One night, his fever and flu-like symptoms were so bad that my husband and I had to take him to the hospital in the middle of the night. We didn't want to take any chances. My mum joined us at the hospital in a taxi. She was also worried about her grandson. After the doctor examined him, she observed that he had a chest infection, so she gave us some antibiotics and sent us off on our way.

Teething

I looked forward to our baby's first set of teeth coming up. But, as with circumcision and immunisation, teething also had its own set of troubles – general discomfort and FEVER! The first time he was teething, I didn't even notice it. He had a temperature that was quite high, and that scared me instantly. Although his gum didn't show any signs of teething, our family doctor asked us to buy "Auntie Mary's Teething Mixture", and it worked like magic. In no time, his temperature was back to normal and he was a lively boy again. Sure enough, a few days later, his first two teeth popped out.

Chapter Seventeen

MUMMY POLICE

This book wouldn't be complete without a chapter on the group of people I call, "Mummy Police". You see, the social commentary didn't end with pregnancy. Now that I had a baby, people felt the need to give unsolicited advice on how I could take better care of him. This was not only annoying, but also insulting. Again, no topic was off-limits for the Mummy Police. They needed to have details of every aspect of my life.

"Did you have a vaginal birth?"

In the days and weeks following childbirth, some people were curious to know how my son had been born. Why did they care? Apparently, some people think that only women who have vaginal births, have experienced the real deal. Anything short of that – caesarean section or vaginal birth with epidural was simply a shortcut to motherhood.

"Your baby is troublesome"

I soon learned that despite the importance Ghanaian

society places on child bearing, it is not a very child-friendly society. Babies are adorable as long as they are quiet. The moment they begin to make any sound – be it a whimper or a loud cry – they instantly lose their cuteness. That's when the commentary begins, "Is he always like that?" "He's troublesome o" "How do you manage?" "That's how baby boys are" and on and on and on and on.

Ironically, I heard these comments most when I was in church. Whatever happened to Jesus' words, "Let the children come to me …?" For some reason, some adults forget that crying is a baby's primary form of communication. Babies cry to communicate their discomfort. So, concluding that my baby is troublesome just because he is crying is rash and insensitive. The most irritating aspect of this was that the commentators never bothered to help me out. They simply informed me that my son was a nuisance and then went on their normal business. How rude?!

"Your baby is fat"

These days even babies have a social responsibility to be the perfect weight. You can't be too skinny- that would mean that your mother is inexperienced and is starving you. Neither can you be too chubby – that would mean your inexperienced mother is overfeeding you.

Some of the comments people made included "What

do you feed him?" and "Obolo". While some of the comments were harmless, others such as "He's fat just like you" were just plain rude and insensitive. What happened to the term "bouncing baby boy"?

"When are you having baby number 2?"

I was first asked this question when our son was only four months old. Some people advised me to "Get on with it" "Don't wait too long" "Hurry and finish with childbearing". I was astonished. I had barely adjusted to my new role as a mother and now people were asking for another baby. Were they already bored with Baby Yaw?

It was hard to please everyone. It seemed that there was always something else to aspire to obtain. Now that I had a child, I needed to have more children as soon as possible. There was no space to relax and enjoy the moment.

"You're Still Fat!"

Some people took their Mummy Police jobs very seriously and were quick to point out to me that I still hadn't lost the baby weight. This was by far the comment that upset me the most. It was annoying that people who had no idea of what I was going through as a new mother, would make insensitive comments about my weight.

Sometimes, I broke down into tears when I heard

such comments. But my mother always consoled me and told me not to pay attention to anyone. She explained that most people didn't mean to offend me with their comments. In fact, for some people, talking about my weight was simply small talk.

Do It My Way

While it is true that as a first-time mother, I often needed some advice on how to take care of my baby, the influx of unsolicited advice was overwhelming. Everybody felt they had timely advice for me. Don't hold him that way, Don't hold him, Leave him, Cuddle him, Sing to him, Read to him, Wean him, Give him Tom Brown, Give him Porridge, Breastfeed him until he's two years.

Who was I supposed to listen to?

Sometimes, I wanted to tell everyone to be quiet and allow me to learn on the job. Yes, mothers usually have a lot of experience on how to take care of children. But every child is unique. So, what works for one child may not necessarily work for another child, so people simply need to take it easy and allow new mothers to learn on the job. After all, in spite of my 'inexperience' as a mum, I still know my son better than anyone else.

Chapter Eighteen

NANNY DIARIES I

Taking care of a baby is hard work, and very few people can do it singlehandedly. My husband worked full-time and also went to school in the evenings after work. So, although he wanted to be a hands-on dad, he couldn't be at home all the time.

We needed a nanny to help with childcare. Fortunately, I already had a nanny. We had worked with her in the past with my two nieces and were confident that she would do a good job with Nana Yaw. Due to her age and experience with children, I had high hopes that she would take care of us, just like my own mother would. I envisaged a relationship where she would take care of not only Nana Yaw, but all of us.

In Ghana, it is common practice for a woman to go to her mother's house, or have her mother move in to stay with her for a few months to assist with childcare. But in my case, Nana Yaw was born at a time when my mother had to be at the office to address some crucial issues that could potentially jeopardize our family business, if not handled urgently. So, I convinced her not to move in with me to help me take care of him. I assured her that with the nanny around, I would be well-taken care of, so she didn't have to worry.

That was wishful thinking. Working with the nanny was a nightmare. After nights of marathon breastfeeding sessions and very little sleep, I was always exhausted in the mornings. However, the nanny didn't report to work until sometime after 8:30am. When she arrived, she was more interested in her breakfast than with giving me a hand. By the time she had finished with breakfast and was ready to help me out, I could no longer fall asleep.

She was also absent-minded and didn't focus on her work. For instance, she could be on the phone for a long time while at work. She could also fall asleep within the twinkle of an eye. Imagine my shock when I left Baby Yaw in her care, so I could rest for a bit, and I came back to the living room only to find her fast asleep while he was still in her arms. What if she had dropped him?

It was obvious that my wish for a helpful nanny had gone out the window. In fact, most of the time, having her around was rather a burden to me. It was like having an extra person to take care of. I had to provide her with her meals (that wouldn't have been a problem if I wasn't so tired all the time), and she also expected me to keep her company! As if that wasn't enough trouble, she also wanted me to change my TV habits to accommodate her favourite programmes. I couldn't take it anymore. This arrangement was simply not working, so I decided to get a live-in nanny who would be able to help me in the early hours of the morning when I needed help the most.

Chapter Nineteen

MATERNITY LEAVE

In order to have three full months of maternity leave with my son, I went to work until the day before my son was born. The term 'maternity leave' is deceptive. When a person is on leave, the person is assumed to be taking a break from work and spending time relaxing or doing something fun. In that sense of the word, maternity leave is in fact no leave at all. It is merely an absence from regular work. Essentially, during my maternity leave, I didn't have to be at my 8 – 5 job, but I had to work around the clock to take care of my new-born son. So, it was no leave at all. Indeed, being on maternity 'leave' was often more tiring that being at 'work'.

In my case, although I was away from the office, I couldn't stop thinking about my work. I was constantly in touch with my colleagues to ensure that everything was going on well. As a Manager, I felt bad that I had to be away from the office for three months, so I tried to work from home as much as possible. Although my boss (my mum) had no expectations of me during that time, I felt like I was letting the team down by being away for so long.

Besides, there were some pressing issues that simply couldn't wait until after my maternity leave had ended.

So, when my baby slept during the day, I would take the opportunity to do some office work and email it to them at the office.

This was against the 'rules', as everyone warned me to sleep when my baby slept, but that was easier said than done. Moreover, afternoon naps have never been my thing. Way back in boarding school, when siesta was compulsory, I used that time to sew (mostly hemming my friends' uniforms to shorten them), read a book or simply stare into space. It was very very very difficult for me to take an afternoon nap. And when I was able to sleep during the day, it would affect my sleep pattern at night.

So, when my son slept during the day, I did other things. Although I was tired, I wanted to do something more than just sleep. I needed some excitement. In fact, it was during this time that I started working seriously on my event planning business. I did lots of research on event planning. I also watched wedding shows on TV. My company was officially born. I designed templates and timelines for my potential clients. It was indeed an exciting experience. Since my mother's 60th birthday was a few months away, I also planned her thanksgiving service and birthday dinner during this time.

As a new mum, I made a conscious effort not to ignore my wifely duties. My own mum always reminded me that staying at home was not an excuse to be scruffy. So, in the morning, while my mother-in-law gave Nana Yaw a bath, I would also jump in the shower to freshen up. I wanted to be a yummy mummy and a sexy wifey, so I made an effort to dress nicely. Later in the evening, just before my husband got home, I would freshen up again to welcome him home. I tried as much as possible to continue doing the things that I used to do for him before our son was born. I cooked and made sure that he always had a packed lunch for work. I didn't want him to think I was neglecting him because of our son.

So, you see, my maternity leave was spent being a mummy, wife, manager and a budding wedding planner. I was certainly NOT on leave.

Chapter Twenty

BACK TO THE REAL WORLD

I love my son with all my heart, but I looked forward to going back to work. I missed the feeling of accomplishment of checking items off my to-do list at work. I wanted to be part of the office team again. I wanted to wear my work clothes. I couldn't wait to be back in my high heels.

But returning to work wasn't that simple. First, we needed to figure out who would care for our son while I was at work. Before I gave birth, I thought it would be easy to find someone I trusted who would take care of Nana Yaw while we were at work. I didn't want to take him to a **crèche** or day care facility at that young age. I preferred to leave him in the comfort of our home. However, that was no longer an option, as I didn't have anyone I could trust to care for my son while I was away. I shuddered as flashbacks of the first nanny falling asleep with Nana Yaw in her arms, ran through my mind. After that incident, I was sceptical about leaving my baby with anyone else. I imagined them falling asleep and dropping my precious boy. So, although my second nanny was doing well, I couldn't risk leaving him in her care unsupervised.

My only other option was to go to work with Nana Yaw and the nanny. Once I got to work, we'd all go into my office (which I share with my mum) and say hello to her. The nanny would take Nana Yaw to an empty office, so I could concentrate on my work. Although I tried my best to work hard, it wasn't easy. Firstly, I was sleep-deprived and could hardly focus. I needed to do nothing but sleep. Secondly, I had to take breaks in between my work to breastfeed Nana Yaw. Usually, by the time I went back to my work, I would have lost my chain of thought. It was extremely frustrating to not be able to operate at my full capacity at work. Besides, having a travel cot and a baby at work made our office look more like an extension of a nursery, than an office.

Although I had officially resumed work, with a baby in tow, it bothered me that I was performing way below my normal capacity. I felt like I was being a slacker. Attending meetings and other events outside the office was extremely challenging. In such instances, I would leave Nana Yaw with the nanny in the car while I attended to business.

A particularly stressful time was during one of our graduation ceremonies at the National Theatre. Unfortunately, my nanny was part of the graduating class, so she had to be inside the auditorium. As the Programme Coordinator, I needed to be on site early enough to make sure that everything was in order. So, we set off very early to beat the rush hour traffic. I needed to be part of the faculty procession, so I gave Nana Yaw to one of the students and quickly walked up to the front of the auditorium. But instead of sitting with the rest of the staff, I had to sneak through the side exit to go for Nana Yaw. We spent the rest of the time in the lobby breastfeeding, supervising ushers, breastfeeding, supervising security, changing diapers, greeting parents, breastfeeding. It was intense. At the end of the ceremony, I was glad it was over. But I was also sad that I couldn't be part of it all. I wish I didn't have to choose between taking care of my son and working.

Another challenge about getting back to work was my wardrobe. For some reason, I hadn't even thought of what I would wear after childbirth. I assumed I would automatically shrink back to my pre-pregnancy size and fit back into my old clothes. But that didn't happen. So, while my maternity clothes were too big, my 'regular' clothes were also too small. I was in limbo. Fortunately, a few of my old clothes still fit (somewhat) so I rotated them. It was so bad that workers at the laundry actually had the nerve to tell my husband that my pink jacket (my favourite office attire) was fading because I wore it too often.

I needed a new wardrobe urgently. However, since I had been out of the country for five years, I had no idea where I could get quality and affordable work clothes to buy in Ghana. I wondered where all my schoolmates shopped for clothes. Surely not everyone travelled abroad for shopping! Luckily, I was able to buy about three new blouses at a store close to my workplace. But they didn't have a wide variety to choose from so I still had to try to squeeze into my old clothes. One of my skirts had become so tight that the inner lining ripped. I was literally bursting at the seams. My fashion style was on a downward spiral. This was definitely not how I planned to make a comeback at the office.

Same old me?

I wanted to be the same person I was before I got pregnant. I didn't want motherhood to change me. I wanted to be the same old me. Looking back, I now realize how irrational I was. I had longed to be a mother for so long, and when I became a mum, I still wanted to have the same lifestyle as I did before my son was born. Unbelievable! But at the time, that was all I wanted. I didn't want people to think that I had become boring because I was now a mother. I wanted to be funky. I wanted to be strong. I wanted to be the ideal working mum.

So, in spite of all the challenges I was going through, juggling with a career, motherhood, marriage and a side hustle, I wanted to be strong and independent. What made matters worse was that other people expected me to be back to my pre-pregnancy self too. During my six-week appointment, my doctor told me that I should be back at my pre-pregnancy weight and ready to resume my normal activities. I know that he meant well. He wanted me to make an effort to lose weight and not be complacent with my physical appearance. He had probably seen too many women who became sloppy after childbirth. But I was overwhelmed by all the pressure. I needed to go back to the old me as soon as possible.

So, although I was surrounded by people who loved me dearly and were ready to help me, I didn't ask for help even when I needed it desperately because I didn't want to appear weak. When I started to feel pain at the site of the caesarean section, I kept quiet until it became unbearable. When I could barely sleep at night because I had to breastfeed countless times, I kept quiet about it. I assumed it was part of motherhood, so I put up a brave front and pretended everything was fine. I didn't want any facet of my life to suffer because I had become a mother. I was more concerned about how people perceived me, than I was with taking care of myself. All was not well with me. I was stressed. I was working a triple shift as a mother, a wife and a working woman.

Losing It

My body could no longer take all the stress. So, one afternoon, on the 19th of December 2012, when I was at work, the whole office started spinning in circles. I had never been so dizzy in my life. I called out to my mum, and she rushed me to the nearest hospital. My son and the nanny followed in another car. On the way to the hospital, I was terrified. What if something happened me? What would happen to my son? Who would take care of him? For the first time in my life, I realized that someone needed me to live. I needed to stay alive for my son's sake. He needed me.

At the hospital, I was immediately taken to the emergency room, where the doctor observed that my blood pressure was very low. That was not a good sign. I was under so much stress that my body couldn't take it anymore. My body was literally shutting down. It was then that I confessed to my mother that I was overwhelmed. I had so much going on in my life that I could barely keep up. I wasn't as strong as I wanted everyone to believe. My mum was extremely sad that I hadn't told her about my struggles earlier. I realized that I had to relax and stop keeping up appearances. My family didn't need me to be perfect. I didn't have to be super woman. I just had to stay alive.

After I was discharged from the hospital, I spent the next few days at my parents' house recuperating. The medication I had been prescribed made me sleep a lot. I didn't like it at all. It made me feel extremely slow and sluggish. I felt like I gained five kilos in five days. In addition to all my health issues, I still had to breastfeed Nana Yaw during the night, and that sort of defeated the purpose of having to rest to recover fully.

Although I enjoyed resting at my parents' house, I looked forward to spending Christmas at home with my son and husband. It was our son's first Christmas and we wanted it to be special. So, in the evening of Sunday, December 23, 2012, with much persuasion, my parents reluctantly 'discharged' me to go back home for Christmas. They were concerned that I would over-exert myself again, but I assured them that I wouldn't lift a finger. I was going to take good care of myself.

Chapter Twenty One

NANNY DIARIES II – DUMPED

A few days before Christmas, our nanny left to spend the holidays with her family. We had agreed that she would spend Christmas with her family and come back to spend New Year with us. Since I was still recuperating at my parents' house when she left, I was unable to give her a special Christmas gift. So, I gave her the Christmas package that I had received at work – a bag of rice, a gallon of oil, and some other food items – for her to share with her family. I intended to get her something nice for the New Year.

On the day that she was supposed to return from her Christmas break, we neither saw her nor heard from her. I was worried. My instincts told me that she wouldn't come back, but I didn't want to believe it. So, we called her to find out if she was returning. She explained that she was on admission at the hospital, but she would resume work the following week. I knew in my heart of hearts that she was telling lies, but I still managed to hold on to a glimmer of hope that she would come back to us.

On the morning of the new rescheduled date, I tried not to think about whether or not she'll show up. Fortunately, we were busy visiting friends and family that day, so I didn't have much time to worry about whether or not she would return. When we got home later that evening, she was still not back. I called her several times, but she did not answer her phone. Later, she sent me a text that read, "I'm not coming back. Sorry for the inconvenience". I couldn't believe it. I was stunned. I had just been dumped.

That night, I cried my eyes out. I had taken her in as a sister and had done my best to make her comfortable. She had never complained to me about her working conditions. As far as I was concerned, she was happy with the job. What made things worse was that she didn't have the courtesy to tell me in person. I was deeply hurt. I felt bad for myself and for my son. It seemed nobody wanted to help us out. I felt betrayed.

As an employer, I had gone out of my way to make her comfortable. But my kindness had not only been thrown back at me, it had also been trampled upon and crushed into the ground. I swore to myself that I wasn't going to let anyone hurt me so much again. I decided to wait a while before taking a new nanny. I didn't want people to keep coming in and going out of our lives.

I kept playing back the last three months over in mind, trying to pinpoint exactly what had made her leave. She had quickly formed a bond with Nana Yaw (something the first nanny couldn't do). During my first meeting with her, I explained to her that I needed someone long term as I didn't want to keep changing caregivers. She assured me that she could do the job. In fact, she wanted to do more than I was asking her to do. She offered to cook, do some house chores and even go to the market to shop for me, but I declined, explaining that I wanted her to focus on helping me to take care of my baby. I didn't want to burden her with too much. I was desperate for her to stay so I pampered her. She had the weekends off, I provided her with meals, and I also took care of her medical bills. And now this was how she paid me back? I couldn't believe it.

Then I blamed myself. Maybe if I had been friendlier or more lenient, she would have stayed. I was heartbroken. I had had two nannies in the short span of six months. That was not the way I had imagined it.

Chapter Twenty Two

WORKING MOTHER

Here I was with a six-month-old baby, a demanding job and no nanny. I had to figure out a way to care for my baby while I attempted to get some office work done. For the first few weeks of being without a nanny, I stayed at home with my son. Whenever he slept or was preoccupied with his toys, I would do some office work. But this didn't always work out very well. Some days, I was able to get a good amount of work done, but on other days, I could barely complete any office tasks.

Although I thoroughly enjoyed being at home with my baby, I felt bad that I was letting my office team down. I yearned to have both worlds - to enjoy time with my baby as well as to get some office work done. I love my baby and I love my job. But it felt like I had to choose one. On the one hand, if I spent too much time on office work it seemed I was abandoning my baby; on the other hand, if I spent time too much time with my baby then it seemed I was abandoning my job. Neither felt right. I needed a balance – a way to give both my son and my job the right amount of care and attention.

So, I decided to take him to work with me. There was so much work to be done at the office that I simply couldn't stay at home. Besides, Nana Yaw was old enough to play by himself, and I hoped that at work I could get some colleagues to help out from time to time. So off we went, back to work…again.

It was tough! Although he had already warmed up to some of my colleagues, they always brought him back to me when he started to cry, or when they thought he was hungry.

At first, taking Nana Yaw to work worked relatively well. A corner of the office was transformed into a playpen. I traded my office chair for a seat next to him on his play mat. However, as he began to get more mobile, the play mats did not suffice. He wanted to crawl around the whole office, but this wasn't hygienic because people entered with their shoes. Each time he crawled outside the play mat boundary, I would have to carry him back to 'safety', only for him to crawl outside again. It was exasperating. He had outgrown the office playpen.

Sometimes, I carried him at my back so that I could get more work done. Other times, I would let one of my colleagues hold him. But that didn't always work out well. Although I preferred that they would keep him close by, they often wandered off with him. For instance, one hot afternoon, my cousin decided it was the perfect time to take Nana Yaw for a long walk in the scorching sun. I was not amused.

Another time, when I asked of his whereabouts, I was told that he was eating. "Eating?" I hadn't asked anyone to feed him. "What could he be eating?" To my dismay, I learned that a colleague had been 'kind' enough to share her lunch of banku with him. Unbelievable!

The toughest part of taking Nana Yaw to work was when I had an engagement outside the office. As much as possible, I tried to avoid outside engagements, but sometimes, there was no way out. Thankfully, my driver, Thomas, is really good with children, so he would take care of Nana Yaw in the car while I went off to attend to official business. However, I could never really concentrate on official business while my son was in the car. I felt guilty. What if something happened to him and they really needed me? I felt as if I was putting work before my son. But I didn't know what else to do. I was frustrated.

I couldn't take it anymore. I needed another solution. Where else could I take him? I wanted to wait until he was at least one year old before taking him to school, so that wasn't an option. Besides he wasn't even nine months, and even if I wanted to take him to school, they won't offer him admission until he was nine months and had finished with all his immunisations. I was at my wits' end. I was stressed, and it showed. I was irritable, and I exploded at the least provocation. I was also extremely emotional and broke down into tears easily. Something was not right.

One day, shortly after I got home from work with Baby Yaw, I received a call from my sister saying, "Awura, Nana Yaw is starting school next week. I've spoken to the headteacher and the proprietress of the school and they have agreed to admit him although he's only eight months. I told them that if they didn't take him, you would die". I was extremely grateful to my sister. This was the best news I had heard in a while.

I was happy that Nana Yaw had been given admission into pre-school, but I felt terribly guilty for shoving him off to school so early. I felt as though I was shirking my responsibilities as a mother. But I knew deep down in my heart that I needed a break. It would be a huge relief to have a few hours to myself every morning to get some rest and to also have undivided attention while I worked. Why did it have to be so hard? I had never imagined that being a working mother could be so difficult.

Chapter Twenty Three

SCHOOL BOY

On the first day of school, my husband and I took him to school together. Although his office was on the other side of town, he wanted to be there when our son walked into his 'classroom' for the first time. I braced myself for a crying episode. I expected him to cry and cling to our legs, begging us not to leave him in a strange place, but he didn't shed a tear. Later, the teacher told us that he cried after we left, but he settled down eventually.

Fortunately, Nana Yaw adjusted well to school. In fact, he seemed to enjoy it a lot – playing with all the toys and having other children around. He also got attached to one of his teachers, Mrs Torsoo. I believe that she was the reason why he didn't cry when we dropped him off at school. He liked her very much and seemed very comfortable and at ease when he was with her.

New Schedule

Now that Nana Yaw was in school, we had a new schedule. Between 8:30 am and 2:30pm, when he was at school, I worked hard to get a lot done at the office. What a difference! With undivided attention, I was more efficient. I was truly back at work.

At 2:30 pm, I would pick him up from school. I always wanted to be the first parent to pick up her child after school. Somehow, it made me feel less guilty for taking my baby to school at such an early age. I prayed that he wouldn't get so attached to his teachers and school friends that he would forget me.

Thankfully, he was always happy to see me when I picked him up. As soon as we got in the car, he would pat my breast, signalling that he wanted his milk. O boy! Not even six hours at school could make him forget about his breast milk. So, I would breastfeed him until he fell asleep or until we got home (whichever came first).

When we got home, I took off my 'career woman' hat, and put on my 'mom' hat. I was on to my second shift of the day. Usually, my first task was to take Nana Yaw's clothes off the drying line. If he was still asleep at this time, I would put him in his cot, so I could iron the clothes. But if he was awake, I would carry him at my back while I ironed. After ironing, I would wash the cups, bowls, etc that he had taken to school. Then I would pack his bag for the next day. By the time I finished with my chores, it would be dinnertime. I know that as a good mother I was supposed to prepare home-cooked meals for him – porridge, pasta, rice balls, banku, etc. But I simply didn't have the strength. So, I took the shortcut and bought bottled food instead. It was a much simpler option. Besides, if he didn't like the flavour I chose that day, all I had to do was to try another flavour the next day.

Dinnertime was often hard work. Since we hadn't yet invested in a high chair, I improvised with his pushchair. I would strap him in the pushchair, turn on the TV to Mickey Mouse Clubhouse, and then proceed to feed him. Ideally, I would love for him to eat everything in the bottle, but that didn't always happen. I needed him to eat well so he could stay asleep throughout the night without waking up for a feed in the middle of the night. But after cooing and mimicking all the cartoons that I could think of, I didn't always succeed in getting him to finish all his food.

The highlight of my evening was undoubtedly the moment my mother-in-law returned home after work. The sound of her car horn was music to my eyes. Her arrival meant that I could take a break. She would take Nana Yaw to her room to play. Later, she would give him a bath and take him to her room to play some more. By that time, I would also be ready for bed. I would then go for him and breastfeed him before bed.

Health Issues

Barely a week after Nana Yaw started school, on Independence Day, I had another health scare, which was even worse than the first episode. I had woken up around 4 am to use the bathroom and realized I could barely stand. The room was spinning very fast in circles. I waited for a while to see if the dizziness would clear up by itself, but it didn't.

So, I woke my husband and told him about my condition. When we called our family doctor, she asked us to come to the hospital immediately. I could barely walk so my husband and our housekeeper had to carry me into the car. We left Nana Yaw in the care of my mother-in-law and headed to the hospital. I didn't know what was happening to me. I was helpless.

At the hospital, the doctor noticed that my blood pressure was low, just like the first time. So, she requested that I run a few tests. But first, I was detained at the ward for a few hours. I also had to check my blood pressure regularly to make sure that my condition was improving. As I sat in the waiting room at the laboratory, I felt sorry for myself. I was sad that I missed the Independence Day parade. From childhood, I always look forward to watching the parade each year. As long as I'm in Ghana, I wouldn't miss the parade for anything. Now here I was, spending Independence Day at the hospital.

Jitters

Although I was happy that Nana Yaw could be in a safe place while I worked during the day, I often worried that something could happen to him while he was at school. So, whenever I received a call from the school, my heart would skip a beat. Thankfully, my office is just five minutes away from the school so at least I wasn't too far away.

Once his teacher called me to inform me that he had a high temperature. The school had a nurse, so I knew that they would only call me if it had persisted. In fact, they were having difficulties reaching me at first, so they called my sister instead. When they finally got through to me, I rushed to the school with my mother. By the time we got to the school, my sister was already there, and she had sponged him in the bathroom. I was so touched by her actions. It was really heart-warming to see how she and my mother had stopped everything they were doing to attend to Nana Yaw. My support system was tight. Truly, it takes a village to raise a child.

School activities

I was a very proud mum at Nana Yaw's first school event. It was their annual sports day. Although he wasn't feeling too well, I didn't want to miss the sports day, so I took care of him at the office that morning. Then, later in the afternoon, when he was well-rested, I took him to school for his sports day.

Although I have attended many school events to watch my nieces, it felt extra special to be at an event as a mother.

I am grateful that he attends a school that makes an effort to engage parents at least once every term through fun events such as sports day, career day, festival of nine lessons and carols, and graduation. Although some parents view these events as a bother, I enjoy them because they give me an opportunity to see how my son interacts with his peers and his teachers.

Nana Yaw is also part of the Taekwondo group at his school, and I love to see the excitement on his face when he wears his Taekwondo uniform and shows us his moves at home.

School Holidays

After a couple of months of enjoying being in school, we were faced with the reality of school holidays. Thankfully, his first school break was for Easter and it was only three weeks, so it was manageable. The real challenge was the long vacation, which was almost three months long. How on earth were we going to engage him during that time. Even if I took my leave during that time, there would still be two more months of his holidays.

My mother came up with a plan – God bless her! She always seems to have the solution to all my problems. She hired a teacher to come home during the holidays to help take care of Nana Yaw and my nieces, Jessie and Marie. This plan worked out remarkably well. With the teacher at home with the kids, they had some structure to their day, even though they were on holidays. She planned fun activities for them that I could probably never have thought of. The only catch was that instead of dropping him off at the school, which was just five minutes away from my office, I now had to drop him off at my parents' house, which was about thirty minutes away from work. Still, I was grateful that my mother had come up with an amazing plan to keep him engaged throughout the three-month school holiday.

Chapter Twenty Four

FIRST HAIR CUT

Nana Yaw's first haircut gets a whole chapter because it taught us a big lesson. By the time he was 7 months old, his hair had grown into an afro, but he still had a bald line running across the back of his head.

One Saturday morning, Daddy took out his clippers and decided it was time for Nana's first haircut. His hair had become difficult to comb and it was also uneven, so we were convinced it was time for a haircut. I was excited. It was another milestone to celebrate. Our baby was growing every day.

Let's just say that Nana Yaw didn't enjoy his first haircut at all! In fact, he cried throughout the 'ordeal'. The buzzing sound of the clippers probably scared him too. So, while we were taking a video of this historic moment, and feeling quite accomplished as parents, he was crying his eyes out.

We went ahead with the haircut because we thought that was the best thing to do. Several people had told us that we needed to cut the 'baby hair' to make way for healthier hair to grow. So, we were actually doing him a favour by cutting his hair. Unfortunately, as the days and weeks went by, the so-called healthy hair didn't appear. Instead, his hair seemed to be getting thinner and thinner each passing day. The head that used to rock an afro, had now been taken over by patches of hair.

Was it because of the haircut? I felt terrible! We should have just left the afro. What if his hair never grows back? Some friends asked us to cut it again. They explained that sometimes the baby hair was stubborn and needed two haircuts before the healthy hair could grow. I didn't budge this time. I had been deceived the first time, so I wasn't going to listen to any hair 'expert' again. I tried to cover his hair with a hat, but he hated it. As soon as I put the hat on his head, he would run his hand over it and take it off.

The morale of this story is that the baby 'experts' are not always right. What works for one child may not necessarily work for another child.

Chapter Twenty Five

OUT AND ABOUT

As much as I longed to go out once in a while, going out with my son was not a simple process. I couldn't decide on the spur of the moment to pop outside briefly to run some errands. No, no, no! Going out with my baby needed a lot of planning.

I'm a planner and a perfectionist, so for a typical outing, my diaper bag would have the following items:

- 5 extra diapers
- 1 pack of wipes
- Vaseline (to prevent diaper rash)
- 1 extra set of clothes
- 1 more set of clothes (in case the first back-up set also got messed up)
- 1 pyjamas set (in case we got stranded and had to spend the night)
- 1 towel (you never know when baby would need a bath)
- Cot sheet (to carry him at my back if needed)
- Paracetamol syrup (just in case baby started teething while we were out)

- Bowl
- Spoon
- 3 feeding bottles
- 1 small tin of SMA
- Biscuits
- 2 packs of juice
- 1 bottle of water
- 1 sippy cup

Yeah so, I pretty much packed a mini closet each time we went out. I wanted to be ready for any unforeseen developments. That's not all though. I also have an emergency bag already packed in my car. So, each time we go out, we have enough to last us for at least a week. Better safe than sorry .

First Kids' Party

I was excited when we were invited to our first kids' party. It was a big step. I would finally be a bona fide guest, and not just another adult trying to gatecrash a kids' party. Although Nana Yaw was only three months, I was hopeful that he would have a good time.

But it turned out that he didn't enjoy it one bit. First of all, the party was taken over by adults (as is usually the case), so there wasn't enough space for everyone. We were pretty much all squished together. The place was so crowded that I didn't feel comfortable breastfeeding (even with a cover-up). So, I had to go out to a corner of the parking lot to breastfeed. Secondly, the bathroom was miles away from the party grounds. So, when Nana Yaw needed a diaper change, I had to go back to the car. Between breastfeeding and diaper changes, we spent quite some time away from the party. What I thought would be a day of fun turned out to be a disaster. I was so tired and stressed out that I wished I had never gone out in the first place. So even before food was served (and that took hours!) we said our goodbyes and headed back to our home sweet home.

Church

One of my least favourite places to go with my son was my church. Oh dear! I dreaded Sunday mornings with a passion. I always looked for an excuse to miss church. Just the thought of going to church was enough to stress me out. Since Jesus said, "Let the children come to me for theirs is the kingdom of God …" I expected church to be the most child-friendly zone. Unfortunately, there was no room for babies in my church.

In fact, I realized church wasn't 'baby-friendly' even before my son was born. During the third trimester of pregnancy, when I had to pee a hundred times a day, I couldn't stay throughout the service because the washrooms were a MESS! So, to avoid any unsightly scene that could potentially traumatize me for life, I boycotted the washrooms altogether! One time, my husband and I had to leave church early just because I needed to pee very badly. Since I couldn't predict the length of the service and my ability to hold in my pee, it was better for me to stay at home and watch TV, at least until our son was born.

When my son was born, we stayed at home for the first three months. By the fourth month, I was ready to be back in church. Getting ready to be on time for the first service was a struggle. But most of the time, we managed to get there before the sermon began.

Once in church, I could hardly concentrate on what was going on. I silently prayed that Nana Yaw would not cry. I didn't need people turning back to see which irresponsible mother couldn't keep her baby quiet during the service.

I also hated having to breastfeed him in the full glare of the 'public'. Yes, I attempted to cover up with my cot sheet, but with the heat, I couldn't possibly cover his head fully to ensure 100% coverage. Besides, he wasn't fond of the cover, so sometimes he would even yank it away, exposing my goodies to the whole congregation .

Nana Yaw didn't seem to enjoy church service either. With all the clapping and singing and heat, after about an hour in church, he would start to cry, and I would have to take him to the back of the church to soothe him. I would carry him at my back and walk up and down to calm him down. All this while, the service would be going on, and I couldn't hear a thing. Why did I even bother going to church?

As I paced up and down with my baby at my back, minding my own business and praying for the service to end, the commentary would start, "He likes crying o", "That's how baby boys are", "Did you think motherhood was easy?", "Now you know how much your mother suffered".

As if I didn't have enough troubles at church, there was no diaper changing station there either. So, when I had to change his diaper, I would have to go to the back of the church again and change his diaper while balancing him on my lap. What happened to a changing station? Was that too much to ask for?

I missed my church in Grand Rapids, Michigan - Grand Rapids First, where we had a special room for mothers of babies and small children. A screen was connected so that the mothers and their children could watch and listen to the church service. It was a baby zone, so mothers could pace up and down to put their little ones to sleep, while listening to the sermon. It was a great environment that showed that the church understood that mothers with babies couldn't be confined to a pew throughout the service.

Valentine's Day

When we first got married, my husband and I started a tradition of going out to our favourite restaurant for dinner on Valentine's Day. The first time, I was pregnant, so we didn't have anything to worry about. It was quite romantic – our first Valentine's dinner as a married couple.

After our son was born, we didn't want to end our new tradition, just yet. So, we took him along with us. It was really sweet to have our little family together at dinner. I was very proud of our little boy. It was as if he knew how much having dinner together meant to us. He didn't cry. Not once. He sat in his high chair (for the most part) and had fun throwing pieces of food on the floor.

But I was too worried about what other people thought that I couldn't fully enjoy our time together. I was worried that we would be scolded for making a mess. I was worried about what the other diners thought of us. So not long after we finished dinner, we unanimously decided that it was time to go home. Looking back, I wish I had just forgotten about everyone else and enjoyed dinner with my little family.

Baby Fair

Once we attended a baby fair, the one place where I was confident that we will be welcomed.

Unfortunately, it was the worst experience! During the forum, the host actually asked all parents with little children to leave the room because the forum was being recorded for TV and the children were making noise. What? I couldn't believe my ears? Since my husband was a speaker, I thought I could get away with standing at the back of the room, but that wasn't good enough. The hostess kept repeating that all little children had to be taken out.

There was another mother standing at the back with me who was distraught. She had paid to be part of the forum, and now she was being asked to step outside. I just smiled at her, acknowledging her pain. As if that wasn't enough, after the event, our son developed a terrible cold because the air-conditioning in the room had been on full blast.

Whether we were out in church or at a party or out for dinner, there was one major factor that made being with a baby difficult – the looks and comments that other people gave. Before I had a child, I always thought that Ghanaians loved children. In a society where a woman's greatest achievement is motherhood, and where women who don't have children (even if it's by choice) are judged, one would hope that children would be held in high esteem. But I soon found out that that was far from the truth.

There's no room for children. We love children as

long as they are quiet. Just like the saying, "Children are to be seen, not heard". But we forget that it is not normal for children to be quiet all the time.

As a mum, I am constantly amazed at people's impatience with babies who cry. There was no room for second-guessing. The moment my son started to cry, I was expected to identify the cause of his crying and address it IMMEDIATELY! I think because I was a first-time mum, people assumed that I didn't know how to take care of my son. So, when he started crying, the queries would begin, "Give him a dummy", "Leave him alone", "Rub his back", "Give him water", "Give him porridge", "Has he eaten?", "You should feed him", "He needs something more filling than breast milk" and on and on and on and on… I knew that they were more concerned about enjoying some peace and quiet than with relieving my son of his discomfort, so I tried to tune them out and rely on my instincts to do what was best for him.

The worst offenders were women, many of whom were mothers themselves. It was as though they had forgotten what they had been through as young mothers. To be fair, not everyone was mean. In fact, some people were very understanding, and would offer to help me out. But sadly, such acts of kindness were few and far between.

Meanwhile, as people glared at me and chastised me for making my baby cry, I would be engrossed in a guessing game, trying to figure out why he was crying. I used the elimination method to find out the cause of his discomfort. Was it hunger? A wet diaper? Heat? Noise? Fatigue?

The reality of motherhood is that I can no longer predict how an outing will go. Will I accomplish all I set out to do? Or will I have to take breaks in-between to soothe a crying baby? I have come to accept that it's a tough world for parents and their babies. People don't love children as much as they make us believe. It's all a façade. They love children only when children are quiet.

Chapter Twenty Six

COMING TO AMERICA

Somewhere in February 2013, my sister suggested that we go on a family vacation together with my mum and my two nieces, Jessie and Marie. Initially, I was sceptical about travelling with an eight-month old baby, but the more I thought about it, the more excited I got. I already had an American visa, but I needed to apply for one for Nana Yaw.

He didn't even have a passport yet. So first, my husband got him a passport, then we applied for a visa. Although I was anxious, I was confident that he would get a visa. There was no reason for the American Embassy to refuse his visa application. I had lived in the States as a student for four years, and I left immediately after my studies. I had also been to a few other countries, and had never flouted any immigration rules, so on paper, we stood a very good chance of getting the visa.

On the day of the appointment, luck was simply not on our side. I got into the embassy only to realize that I had left the receipt at home. So, I had to go to the nearest bank to see if they could retrieve a copy from their system. I could as well have gone back home for it as the bank staff were unbelievably slow. They were already busy with other things, and my situation was not an emergency. Finally, they were able to retrieve the data and printed out a duplicate receipt for me. I rushed back to the embassy, praying that we weren't too late to be interviewed.

When we arrived at the embassy, there was only one other person left inside. When we were called to the booth, Nana Yaw was a bit uneasy, so I gave him to my husband while I was interviewed. The interviewer asked a few basic questions, then he passed on our file to a colleague to review. I was worried, but I was still hopeful that we would get the visa. A few minutes later, he returned to the desk, and to my dismay, he refused my baby the visa.

What???! He simply said, "It doesn't make sense to travel with an eight-month old baby". Then he gave the passport back to me and that was it! I couldn't believe it. I struggled to put myself together as we walked back to the car- our walk of disappointment. How could they refuse him? I was stunned!

My initial reaction was to give up. Perhaps, we weren't meant to travel. I was so sad. I felt sorry for my son. I felt like I had let him down. What did I do wrong? How could they refuse a baby whose mother had a valid visa? They were basically trying to tell me to also stay in Ghana.

My sister was furious, and she told me to re-apply. There was no way they were going to the States without me and Nana Yaw. She assured me that we would all go together as family. So, the following day, I purchased another application form and booked a second interview. I wasn't going to give up so easily. I had to fight for my son.

On the day of our second interview, we set off very early in the morning to beat rush hour. I checked and double-checked our documents to be sure that everything we needed was in the file. I was extremely nervous. This was our last shot. It was a Thursday and we were scheduled to travel the following Monday. I prayed fervently to God for favour.

This time around, my husband wasn't allowed to come in with us. That made me nervous because I was worried I'd need help in case Nana Yaw started to cry during the interview. It appeared that the morning interview slots were busier than the afternoon slots, so we had to wait for a longer time before we were called to the booth. When Nana Yaw's name was called, I walked up to the booth with him in one arm, and my handbag and file in the other arm. Guess who was on the other side of the booth? The same man who had refused us the visa during the first interview. He explained that since it had been less than a week since he interviewed us, someone else would have to interview us. So, we went back to our seats to wait to be called again.

I was very nervous. In a few minutes' time, we would know whether or not we would be going on vacation with the rest of the family. Just at that time, I caught a funky smell. I hoped that it was only a fart, but after a few minutes, it was clear that Nana Yaw had done a poo. Really? Talk about bad timing! There was no way, absolutely no way that I was getting out of my seat. What if we were called while we were in the restroom? I didn't want to take any chances this time. So, I remained seated and pretended there was no smell. But the lady sitting next to us had other plans. First, she chose a less direct approach by simply squishing her nose to tell me that my baby needed a diaper change. But I pretended that everything was fine and ignored all her cues. Then she decided to be more direct and told me plainly that I needed to change my son's diaper. But I stayed glued to my seat. If the smell bothered her, she could find another seat because I wasn't going anywhere until the interview was over.

Finally, after what seemed like hours, we were called to the booth again. I said a silent prayer. I needed divine intervention. When the officer glanced through our file on his computer, he began to dismiss us, asking us what could have changed since our initial interview less than a week ago. He reached out to take the refusal letter, but this time, I had learnt my lesson. I wasn't going to be intimidated by anyone. So, I explained to him that at the first interview I wasn't given a chance to explain why we were travelling. Then, even before he could ask me any more questions, I started explaining to him that I had NO desire to live in the United States permanently. I also told him all the countries I had visited. Not once had I overstayed or flouted any immigration rules. Then, I slipped all my documents under the booth to him. I wasn't leaving anything to chance. I was behaving like a crazy lady. I was on a mission. My son needed that visa, and I was going to do all in my power to ensure that he got it. In the end, God answered my prayers, and the interviewer had no option than to give us the visa. I was elated! Our persistence had paid off. I was grateful to my mum, my sister and my husband for encouraging me to reapply for the visa.

From Kotoka to JFK

After our visa application was approved, it was time to pack. I wished my husband could travel with us, but he had just started at a new job and wasn't yet due for annual leave. I was anxious about travelling alone with Nana Yaw. Well, we weren't really alone. But my sister had her hands full with her two daughters, Marie and Jessie, and I didn't want my mum to be stressed helping me with childcare. She needed a lot of rest and I didn't want to take that away from her.

I was most concerned about the flight to America. It was a long journey. It would take about 6 hours to get to London, and another 7- 8 hours to get to New York.

Let me just say that the Kotoka International Airport was NOT child-friendly. First, the ramps inside the airport were so steep that it took some balancing skills to push the pushchair down without falling. Then we got to the boarding gate, where we had to go down the stairs to the shuttle bus, and there was no lift! I couldn't believe it! No lift and no alternate arrangements for mothers with pushchairs. Fortunately, I got a good Samaritan to carry the empty pushchair down the stairs while I walked down with my Nana Yaw. Finally, we got to the foot of the plane and I was told to fold my push chair. Although the lady at the store had taught me how to fold it earlier that day, I simply couldn't remember. Instead of assisting me, the grounds staff was impatient and simply told me that if I didn't fold it, she would have to leave it behind. Fortunately, just before she gave up on me, I figured out how to fold it. Whew!

After expending all my energy on figuring out how to fold the pushchair, I trudged up the stairs to the plane, with the little energy I had left. I couldn't wait to arrive in America. I prayed that Nana Yaw would sleep soundly throughout the flight. Nobody likes to have a crying baby on their flight, so I prayed that we won't be on the receiving end of exasperated stares and evil glares. I didn't even let him cry for breast milk, I offered it freely and willingly. He could suckle as much as he wanted, as long as he didn't cry. The young white lady sitting next to me wasn't too pleased to have me breastfeed so close to her. But that was the least of my worries. If only she knew that by breastfeeding, I was saving everyone on the flight the trauma of having a crying baby on board, she would have thanked me.

Fortunately, the rest of the flight went rather smoothly. During our transit in London, I realized how different life could be as a mother. Usually, when I travelled alone, I enjoyed long transits because they gave me an opportunity to explore the airport. But now, I had a baby in tow and couldn't wait to board the plane for the last leg of our trip. I wanted us to reach our destination within the shortest possible time, because I didn't want him to get too tired from the long trip.

Finally, after over twenty hours of travelling, we touched down in New York. By then, we were all extremely tired and sleepy. We couldn't wait to jump into bed.

Makeover

A few days after we arrived in America, I found out that the real motive for the trip was to get me a new wardrobe. My mum and sister were horrified at my less-than-stylish set of clothes post-child birth, so they were determined to get me new clothes. So, on the first day of shopping, they insisted that I get my clothes first before they even start looking at clothes for themselves. How sweet! I didn't realize that my fashion sense had deteriorated so much. Thankfully,

with the help of my two stylists, I got new clothes
mostly for work and a few for church. I was back on
track to becoming a yummy mummy.

Besides shopping, it was good to be away from
home and work. Being in a different environment
gave me new inspiration and ideas. But I missed my
husband terribly. It was also quite tiring taking care
of Nana Yaw around the clock. He was still waking
up at least twice each night for breast milk, so I was
still tired and sleep deprived. Nevertheless, it was a
lovely vacation. And to think that if I had given up
after the first visa refusal, we would have missed out
on all that fun and excitement!

Chapter Twenty Seven

Free at Last!

About two weeks to Nana Yaw's one-year birthday, I was admitted at the hospital for a stomach infection. I was very worried because we didn't know what was causing the infection. And of course, everyone thought I was pregnant! But I wasn't. Anyway, my hospitalization turned out to be a blessing in disguise because during the two days that I was hospitalized, Nana Yaw finally decided to say goodbye to breast milk.

According to my husband, it was a real struggle. The first night, he cried and cried and cried and cried for breast milk and refused to take the formula. But by the second night, it had become obvious that there was truly no breast milk in sight. He was left with only two options:

Option 1: Starve to death
Option 2: Accept the formula and live!

Thankfully, he chose the second option. I couldn't believe my ears when my husband shared the good news. Nana Yaw had finally parted ways with my boobies. Freedom!!!

Ironically, my new-found freedom wasn't all joy and bliss. First of all, I missed the special bond we shared during breastfeeding. I had lost my magic potion that usually calmed him down or put him to sleep.

Secondly, I experienced a fair amount of pain and physical discomfort. Apparently, my breasts didn't get the memo that breastfeeding was over, so they continued to produce milk, and that left me with painfully over-sized boobs. Initially, I tried to express the milk manually, but I was told that that would actually worsen the situation. The best remedy was to place a warm (or was it cold?) towel on the breasts to alleviate the pain.

Also, the fact that I was no longer breastfeeding didn't mean that the late-night feeds were over. Sadly, even with formula, Nana Yaw continued to wake up at least twice every night for milk. Hmmmmmpppphhhh! So, it turned out that the freedom I had waited so long for, was not freedom at all.

Chapter Twenty Eight

ONE-YEAR OLD

Words can't express how excited I was when Nana Yaw turned one. It was unbelievable. The year had gone by quickly. A lot had happened within a year, and we were thankful to God for staying by our side through the happy and difficult times. Within one year, our family had changed. We had also changed- we were no longer "Yaw and Awura Amma", we were "Yaw, Awura Amma and Nana Yaw".

After one year of motherhood, I had settled into a comfortable routine of childcare. I still didn't have a nanny, but I was managing just fine. Nana Yaw was more active and vocal now, so I enjoyed being with him. He wasn't clueless anymore - he responded to his surroundings, and I loved watching him engage with things around him. Without colic, breastfeeding and house arrest, I was content.

My husband and I were enjoying being parents to Nana Yaw. We looked forward to the birthday celebration. We planned it to be a small party with family and friends who had shared our journey with us. Indeed, it was a blast! Complete with a bouncy

"

castle, face painting, Mickey Mouse, popcorn and lots of exciting games. The kids had fun, and the adults had a good time too. It was a special celebration for me. God had seen me through a very difficult year. Through all the challenges, I learned lessons of patience, endurance, teamwork and total dependence on God. I learned to cherish good health and not to take anything for granted. I was glad to be able to look back on the past year and thank God for allowing me to mature and blossom into a young mother.

The birthday fell on a Friday, so it kick-started a weekend of celebrations. That day, he celebrated with his class at school. Hubby and I, together with my mum, joined him at school for his 'party'. It was such a great feeling to be celebrating my son's birthday. It was a new feeling, and I loved it!

The main birthday party had been scheduled for Sunday. My mum was to prepare most of the food for the party so there wasn't much for me to do. She wanted me to enjoy the celebrations as much as possible, because I had been through a lot in the past year.

On the morning of the party, we took it easy at home. We wanted Nana Yaw to get enough rest, so he wouldn't be tired by the time the guests arrived. I was amazed at all the team effort to bring the party together. With my parents, in-laws, cousins, friends and family around, I didn't have to lift a finger. My main task for the day was to entertain our guests and to make sure everyone had enough to eat and drink.

The birthday party was a huge success. The kids had a lot of fun with the bouncy castle, popcorn, face painting and other exciting activities. The adults were not left out, and they also had a good time.

In the end, I was amazed at all the love our friends and family showed. It exceeded my expectations and I felt blessed to have such a network of people. I was pleasantly surprised at the number of presents Nana Yaw received. We had fun unwrapping presents and guessing who had sent them. What a great way to crown a rather hectic year!